Bunkside Seamanship

Bunkside Seamanship

MIKE LLOYD-JONES

ROBERT HALE LIMITED
LONDON

© *Mike Lloyd-Jones 1978*
First published in Great Britain 1978

ISBN 0 7091 6414 9

Robert Hale Limited
Clerkenwell House
Clerkenwell Green
London EC1R 0HT

PRINTED IN GREAT BRITAIN BY
WILLMER BROTHERS LIMITED, BIRKENHEAD

Dear Mr. Lloyd-Jones.

At last I am finding a few moments to write to you, having read your typewritten script of your book 'Bunkside Seamanship'.

May I say at once how much I enjoyed it. Apart from being written in a lighthearted and readable vein it was full of sound commonsense and good seamanship. I would say that apart from being good reading for the beginner it is also jolly useful to the more experienced yachtsman or the fisherman, or for that matter anyone who goes to sea. I know that I found much that I didn't know or had forgotten. It really is crammed full of facts, written in such a way as to make it very interesting reading.

I do commend this to your publisher as being a book well worth the bookshelf of any would-be sailor or fisherman.

Congratulations on being so dedicated as to produce a book that has obviously cost you many hours in research.

Yours sincerely,

Alec G Rose

Havant.

Contents

Figures and Tables

Author's Note

I am indebted to many for assistance in writing this book; in the first instance to Miss E. Houghton-Brown, of Parkstone, Dorset who helped me to overcome both the physical and the mental effects of (what I found to be) an exhilarating but fairly exhausting war and who, later, helped me to move from Royal Marine Barrack Room to Royal Navy Wardroom. From her also, came my love and deep respect for the power of the sea, which this book is all about.

The loyal help and 'beyond the normal call of duty' patience, forebearance and fortitude of my wife Nancy, combined with her encouragement, has made the writing possible.

Also beyond price has been the scrupulous technical editing by my good friend and colleague in the Sea Cadet Corps, Lieutenant-Commander R. F. Careless, R.N.R. of some material.

The graphic work, particularly of weather, has been greatly enhanced by the artistry of Lawrence G. Richards, and the willing advice on size and duplication of drawings by Rank Xerox Ltd.

It is difficult to name so many names, but I owe an immense amount to the encouragement and enthusiasm received from both the Headquarters and outlying stations of the Royal National Lifeboat Institution, H.M. Coastguard, H.M. Customs and Excise, and last but not least, from Trinity House and her sister services.

Amongst many others, I have received unstinted help from Lord Newborough of Belan Fort; Captain Ellis, Harbour Master of Caernafon; The Edgbaston Observatory of Birmingham

University, British Ropes (Marine) Ltd., Technical Librarians up and down the country and the Birmingham Fire Brigade.

My general reference books have been the basic books for every seaman's bookshelf, the *Admiralty Manuals of Seamanship*, Reed's *Nautical Almanac*, and *The Shell Pilot to South Coast Harbours*.

You will find a detailed index and glossary of terms at the end of the book, which will, I trust, explain any technical words or expressions not immediately clear to you.

I hope that this book will lead you to further reading, not necessarily to make you a slicker, swankier or faster sailor, but if I have shown you the way to become a safe *seaman*, then this book has been worth the writing.

'A book may be amusing with numerous errors, or it may be very dull without a single absurdity'.

Mike Lloyd-Jones.

ONE

Sailor or Seaman?

I once had an ancient relative who quite openly practised genocide for over twenty years. She called it nursing. I also know some sailors who would not make competent skippers of a plastic duck in their baths, far less a vessel at sea. Nursing is to a certain extent similar to boat handling. Often emergencies crop up which previously you would have thought to be beyond your knowledge and capabilities, but you know that you have to deal with them yourself, and nearly always it turns out that it is not so much what you do, but the way in which you do it that results in the good or bad effects on other people or yourself.

In this book I introduce you to some of the very basic aspects of seamanship. Again, like nursing, it is both an art and a science, and apart from the basic problems, one is always faced with the essential human element in the one case, and the equally unpredictable weather element in the other.

This book will not be too erudite or complicated, because I am not very erudite or complicated myself, and if some purists wish to argue with some of my simpler but factual interpretations of complicated problems, so be it.

To get down to facts then straight away, you will notice that in many chapters are sketches of flags of the International Code with a particular letter of the phonetic alphabet, and often the Morse or semaphore signals, and it is these that are of vital importance to safety, and to my mind it is the safety aspect of each and every action taken that makes a *sailor* into a *seaman*.

Ask yourself honestly, would *you* risk losing your life to help a lazy idiot? Yet this is what is happening around our coasts with appalling frequency. Any one of those undaunted men who are literally devoted to the Lifeboat Service could (if they were the types to boast) recount occasions where money was certainly wasted, and worse, where injury or even death was caused to a lifeboatman or a coastguard by an idiot who bought himself a boat and was too ignorant, selfish or lazy to learn how to use it properly. The idiot who forgets to top up and runs out of fuel on a dangerous coast, or one who does not realize the significance of the meaning of the signal 'U' Uniform – 'You are running into danger' which is hoisted by the harbour master while the coastguard is flashing · · – at him. Other idiots have engine failure or sail trouble, and drift into danger because they hadn't the foresight to have an anchor, or else they sail gently into a savage ebb-tide race without even realizing their predicament.

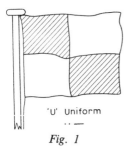

'U' Uniform

· · –

Fig. 1

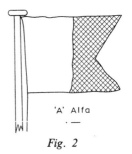

'A' Alfa

· –

Fig. 2

They ignore the flag 'A' Alpha – 'Keep well clear of me at slow speed as I have a diver down'. If you pause for a moment to consider the consequences of cutting a diver's air-pipe or life-line, or hitting him with your prop, or sharp keel, I think you will agree that maiming or death is rather a heavy price for the diver to pay for someone else's ignorance.

In short, these selfish idiots make a confounded nuisance of themselves, and are a menace to others who are quietly enjoying themselves and the freedom of open water, and who have taken the trouble to learn how to allow others to do the same.

There is, of course, more to know about the sea than any one man can learn, even when the sea is predictable, but it is as capricious as a witch – and aren't all ships and boats referred to as 'she' or 'her'?

I suppose that to write about boats, the best place to begin, as in most things, is at the beginning, which should find you having a long, long quiet think about the type of boat which would suit you best, what you want to use it for, who is going to be in it with you, and where will you be going.

You have at least five very basic types of boats to choose from, excluding submarines, 'varsity eights', hovercraft and other specialities, but please always keep in the back of your mind the fact that very seldom is one type of boat suitable for more than a fleeting acquaintance with waters it was not designed or built for. You have (1) the canal or inland waterways type cruiser, barge, or narrow-boat, (2) the light sailing dinghy for lakes, reservoirs, and estuaries, (3) the fast planing speed-boat which is also for lakes and estuaries and limited in-shore use, (4) the small sea-boat for fishing and pleasure trips up and down the coast and into the many inlets and coves, and finally (5) the off-shore sea-boat in which one can cruise even in roughish weather moderately comfortably under sail and or power, and 'going foreign' when skippered by someone with experience, preferably of the local water.

This book is written primarily for the last two types, for the simple reason that the previous three need to know only a few chapters of it, but the man hoping eventually to 'nip over to the Continent for the weekend' should know this book backwards before he starts, and even then he will be just about as vulnerable as a newly qualified driver on the M1 Motorway at peak hour.

Having said that though, owners of the first three categories of boats mentioned above will be all the better for further knowledge of their hobby if they do learn the essentials of seamanship, because when all types of boats are mixed together, as they might well be in the Thames, Severn, Barmouth, Poole, Solent, Hull, the Clyde or any one of a dozen similar stretches of water, they can only handle their boats properly and considerately if they realise the difficulties of those in the other boats.

If your intended course is blocked by a yacht 'in irons,' that is, stationary, head into the wind with her sails flapping wildly, just try to imagine what a twit he feels when he sees you coming towards him. Haven't *you* ever made a mistake and heard sarcastic remarks as you tried your damndest to get it right, and how angry you felt at the unfairness of the rude comments? Most of us have at one time or another.

Reverting to the choice of boat, the type that one finally chooses very often reflects the image of the person one is, rather like many pets get to look like their owners, or is it the other way round? The same is often true of a man's car and the trimmings he has in, on and around it. What sort of pet have you got or would you want, a solid stolid one, or a temperamental but highly intelligent one? Have you one or more wives with associated offspring and or pets who will be sailing with you, or do you simply want to have a try at water ski-ing? Do you want to sail or motor vigorously for an hour or so, then, rather as after a game of squash, have a shower, change, and join the chaps at the bar?

Do you want to cast off late Friday night, sail out of harbour into the darkness, glide quietly into a tiny sheltered cove, 'drop the hook' and savour the silence and the peace? Do you (or your wife) insist on elaborate and sophisticated toilet or cooking facilities and equipment? Can you keep dry, or dry your clothes if wet? Is the speed enough, or is the fuel consumption going to be too heavy, and are the fuel and water tanks and your cable locker big enough for cruising? Is there enough room to stow plenty of clothes for both sea and shore?

These are only a few of the questions you must ask yourself, and find an honest answer to, if you really want to get the best out of your hobby. Boats are not just boats, but are designed for a specific purpose, just as on the roads we have the milk-float, the Bentley, the 'souped-up' mini, the double-decker bus and the petrol tanker. Any one of these would fail doing something which could be carried out perfectly simply by one of the others.

Having got your basic type of boat decided, you still, I'm afraid, have the always very arguable (or discussible) question of sail or motor, or even big sails with small motor, or big engines with small sails, or no sails at all.

The full-blooded, heavily canvassed ocean yacht can be exhilarating with a good crew, but outright dangerous if under-manned or in inexperienced hands, and can be in trouble if with only a minimal engine. The powerful multiple-screw motor-cruiser is dependent only on her engines, and without a sail to steady her she can roll alarmingly in a seaway, and many have no mast for signalling purposes.

While being a purely personal opinion, if you are thinking of any amount of off-shore sailing without a regular trained crew, I would recommend the compromise of a motor-sailer which is designed to give the best possible advantages of both but with the minimum disadvantages of either. This decision will not make you either a 'stick-and-string' man or a 'driver' as the one often disparagingly says of the other.

Your third difficult decision concerns the nature of the hull itself. First, and still available quite cheaply, are wooden boats with their attendant maintenance troubles and costs, although modern two-pot paints have a very good resistance, and if cleaned down, filled with the correct material, and properly done under ideal circumstances, they last well and are easy to free from the inevitable weed and algae.

Alternatively, an acquaintance of mine bought an old lifeboat very cheaply, and although the planking was anything but perfect, the bones of the skeleton were sound so he took it out of the water, and literally using the hull as a mould, laid fibre-glass matting both inside and out, and when completed had a sound maintenance-free glass fibre boat. Be warned, though, the basic framework of the hull was sound and was thoroughly treated with a 'bug and algae' killer before starting work.

Glass-reinforced plastic, is excellent. If you buy the hull and assemble it yourself it works out very cheaply indeed, although I will not go too deeply into certain aspects of G.R.P., as enemies are

B

made in yacht clubs and bars by even suggesting the possibility of cracking under severe storm and impact damage, and possible fire hazards. The trouble is that there is no such thing as 'plastic' as such; the many forms have totally differing advantages and disadvantages and you are very much in the hands of the boat designer and builder with the knowledge, craftsmanship and honesty that he puts into your particular boat, so that the cheapest might not always be the best – but neither necessarily need the most expensive.

One thing to remember about fibreglass and some 'plastics' is that, surprising as it may seem, they can rot. Generally this material is covered with an adhesive finishing coat, and if this is deeply scratched, water can penetrate into the inner layers, algae will enter, the strands inside are forced apart and, when separated, become waterlogged, and in time the whole casing will gradually disintegrate. Always make frequent checks then, for gashes into the fibres and fill them and cover immediately, before the damage spreads.

Steel is probably the ideal for largish vessels, but maintenance and repair is obviously more than a saw, screwdriver and putty-knife job. It needs to be done by a professional as does work on the other popular metal, aluminium, but welding here is very tricky. As with steel, aluminium can in certain cases cause an electro-chemical action to take place under your very nose, and your hull can rot away without you even realising it, unless you take professional advice and preventive measures.

Concrete is much maligned, but I think will come more to the fore as more top designers become interested in ferro-concrete as a medium.

Having decided on your boat then, your very last – and sometimes the most difficult – problem to solve is where are you going to sail it from. If you have a light one with a trailer for your car you have no problems, but if you want moorings, the only thing is to think of the type of sailing you want, and your commuting distance to the boat.

Once you have decided on the area in which you want moorings,

I would strongly recommend you to visit the local sailing clubs, and introduce yourself to your local harbour master, coastguard and lifeboat stations. The reason for this is simply that you will invariably find courtesy and helpfulness once they realize that both you and the boat of your choice are going to be an asset to their water and not a liability, and they will help you as much as they can in all ways.

The remainder of the chapters in this book explain a little more detail of what I have only touched on in this introduction. Having been thus introduced, I trust that you will enjoy reading the rest of it and will grow in confidence and competence as a seaman.

TWO

Time and Tide Wait for No Man

One of life's little perplexities that might or might not have rattled your brain cells up until now is this: 'Why can a Greek in his national costume (if he feels so inclined) stand knee-deep in his local seawater all day long without getting his frilly knickers wet, whereas if a Channel Islander so stood in *his* locality, he would, at times, be more than depressed by the odd thirty feet of salt water above his head?'

Over the last couple of thousand years that this problem has been philosophised over and written about, man has, to a limited extent, mastered the general rules of tidal movements and sea levels which alter so much in quantity, direction and speed in different parts of the world. These can now be predicted with a fair degree of accuracy, (provided one discounts the effects of weather which are predictably unpredictable).

I dislike the pedantic parrot-like learning of terms as much as anybody, and have tried wherever possible to avoid it in this book, but the next paragraph is very important, and the terms in it must never be used loosely.

Tide is the general *vertical* movement of the sea's surface between *high water* and *low water*, and the difference between high and low water is the *range*, and is measured in feet or metres. *Tidal streams* on the other hand are measured in knots, (often two figures are given, one for the speed at Spring Tides and the other at Neaps, which I will explain in a moment). It is these tidal or tide streams which are the definite *horizontal* movements of water which alternately fill and empty our bays and flood or denude our beaches to give high and low water. It is important that you should distinguish between these carefully, because *high tide* and *high water* are only the same thing about twice a month.

Coming back to my examples of Greece and the Channel Islands, why is there such a difference in the two places? It's a simple enough question, but a complicated answer.

Every schoolboy knows that tides are governed by the moon, but as the idea of this chapter is to learn how to find out how much water you've got under the keel of your boat at any place, and any time, we have to go into the basic reasons more deeply. To give you an example of what we are confronted with, east of Guernsey in the Channel Islands is the little French fishing port of Dielette, and the harbour is, I would guess, little over 350 yards square. *That harbour can be dry at noon, covered by nearly 40 feet of water by six p.m. and bone dry again a little after midnight.* This astonishing amount of water pours into and out of the harbour (and believe me, you have quite a mooring problem) but also you very quickly become aware of the incredible amount of power generated by the moon whose speed in orbit around us is about 2,300 m.p.h. and even over the earth immediately below its course is a staggering 930 m.p.h. It needs a very large amount of water for the moon to have an effect, so if a millionaire friend of yours boasts that his inland swimming pool is tidal, I would be inclined to disbelieve him.

We have then, this colossal constant action and reaction on the Atlantic Ocean below, and the Atlantic covers thirty *million* square miles. That's a lot of water to react on, and as the moon travels around the earth in an easterly direction, where is the wave that is caused forced to go to? It is either squeezed between South Africa and the Antartic ice, or swirls into and around the Mediterranean entrance, but has little effect further in, or around the Arctic until stopped by the north polar ice, but, far more important as far as we are concerned, it seeps around Scotland into the North Sea (and the Baltic Sea, where like the Mediterranean it whirls about and comes out again because it has nowhere else to go to) but also forces its way into the English Channel. It is here that our trouble arises, for apart from the weekend sailors and professional fishermen this stretch of water is the busiest sea-lane in the whole world, carrying some 100,000 ships each year. Water is squeezed into the funnel-shaped Channel, which is about a hundred miles wide in the west and only twenty odd in the east towards Dover, and is compressed by the English and French

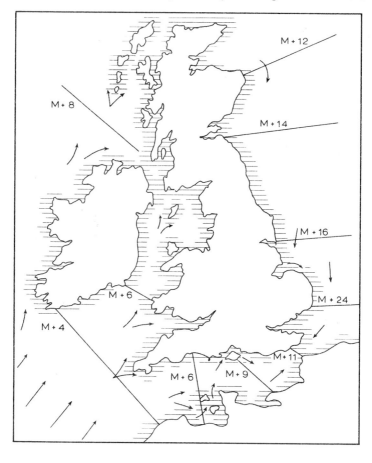

Fig. 3 Tides at 'M' hour

coasts becoming nearer and the depth shallower in the middle. It occasionally produces somewhat startling side effects after bouncing back off projections like the Cherbourg peninsular and swirling around the Channel Islands always trying to catch up with the rest of itself. It goes into whirlpools of relief after elbowing its way around Portland Bill (hence the infamous Portland Race) and then splits into both sides of the Isle of Wight at different speeds with such odd results as causing four tides per day instead of the usual two.

If you imagine the moon's magnetic wave starting way out in the Atlantic at 'M' – Hour you will see from Fig. 3 that it takes about four hours (call it M + 4) travelling eastwards to get near to Land's End where it splits either side eastwards and northwards, takes just over six hours to get up Channel at M + 11, whereas to go right around Scotland and all down the North Sea, the stream meets up with the other half of itself again off the Thames Estuary at M + 24.

Where they meet, incidentally, is the dreaded Goodwin Sands, some parts of which at times can tower some nine feet above the surface, but yet could have twenty feet of water over them at others. The number of ships lost through the ages on what has come to be known as the 'ships' graveyard' must be countless, so please try not to add to them as apart from being a dangerous nuisance to the Lifeboat Service, your wrecked boat causes pollution.

You might find it helpful to really study this sketch and see where the streams travel, and to note the time-scales. The arrows in this sketch are of course reversed every $6\frac{1}{4}$ hours when from Dover the stream belts off down Channel for $6\frac{1}{4}$ hours, waits a short period – slack water – then off up Channel again. Thus, *your next high water will be just under $12\frac{1}{2}$ hours following the last one, and low water half-way* ($6\frac{1}{4}$ hours) depending of course on wind and local factors.

Many people only remember Captain Webb because of the boxes of matches with his picture on the label, but when I tell you that it took the gallant Matthew 21 hours 45 minutes to make his

historic swim from Dover to Calais in 1875, his final plotted
course, sketched in Fig. 4 shows graphically that the effect of
tide streams at Dover, and what it meant to him, means the same
to you over a hundred years later. Boats and people might have
changed but the tidal streams haven't.

The distance, shore to shore, from Dover to Calais is 23 miles,
but in the 21 hours 45 minutes that it took him, he swam in fact 38
miles and was involved in $3\frac{1}{2}$ changes of tidal streams. I can think of
no better example of the tidal effect to show you what would
happen to you if you sailed out of Dover Harbour making (shall
we say to make your course comparable to that of Captain Webb)
$1\frac{1}{2}$ miles per hour, and keeping on a constant bearing of 125 degrees
or thereabouts. In fact a boat with more hull submersed, and
greater above water area for the wind to act upon, would probably
do worse in time than our resolute Captain Webb. However, be
warned about what you take on in your boat in emulating this

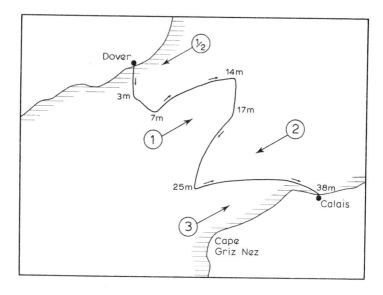

Fig. 4 Captain Webb's Swim

bravery, as he died trying to swim over Niagara Falls. I wouldn't do that, if I were you.

Before going into the advantages and disadvantages of these tidal streams and the different ranges, how do we know where they are and when? There are several publications, some privately published, available through bookshops or yachting papers, or there is the Admiralty (or should I say Ministry of Defence–Navy) which publishes several editions available from H.M. Stationery Office. Those covering the Channel and the surrounding area work on the six hours before and after high water at Dover, and they show the direction of the tidal streams at each hour, and alongside the arrow is the speed in knots.

A knot is the speed of one nautical mile in one hour, the nautical mile being taken officially as 6,080 feet. The remainder of the table is simple enough to remember if you start at the bottom end, that is the fathom. There are 6 feet to a fathom, 100 fathoms to a cable, and 10 cables to one nautical mile. Ah, some bright bloke says, '6 × 100 × 10 is 6,000 not 6,080'. The only answer I can give to that is that this book is about boats, not swimming, and provided you are not swimming, who gives a hang for the odd 80 feet?

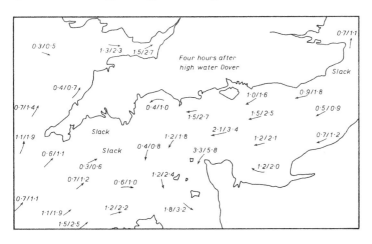

Fig. 5

Looking at the arrows showing the tidal streams, you will see that there are two figures alongside them, one denoting the average expected speed at spring tides, the other lesser number the speed at neap tides, which are when the moon's effect is greater and less respectively. The effect of spring tides, which occur roughly every fourteen days is that the pull is greatest between $1\frac{1}{2}$ and 2 days after *full* and *new* moons, when both the speed of tide streams and the range is greatest, while they are least at neap tides, that is at a quarter and three-quarter moons. So if you are determined to do a voyage of discovery up a shallow creek, don't do it at high water springs, or if you go aground, you might stay there for a fortnight.

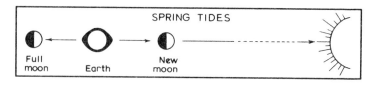

Fig. 6 Effect of Moon and Sun on tides

The effect of spring and neap tides is complicated further by the fact that the moon's circuit around the earth is oval, and when nearest to us, there is an *extra* pull, called perigee tides, and corresponding lesser effect when the moon is further away in its orbit, known as apogee tides. Finally in this depressing lot of technicalities—don't worry, you'll see the advantages later on—the sun also has an effect by the earth's oval orbit around *it* and has greater effects still at the equinoxes (equal nights) on 21st March and 23rd September.

Well, now that you've got this information, how do you handle it?

Your chart has figures all over it, showing 'Chart Datum' depths, which are the lowest to which the water is *ever* likely to drop at that point. If we look at it 'fish-eye-view' we would get something like this:

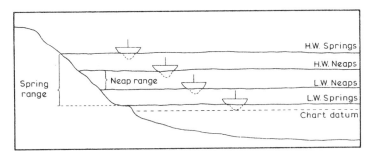

Fig. 7 Fish-eye View of Tidal Ranges

A set of tide tables, a portion of which is illustrated later, will give you times of high water and the range in feet between them for each day of the year at all the major ports, together with corrections to add or subtract to give you the smaller creeks and harbours between them.

You use the tide tables with a simple bit of arithmetic known as 'the twelfths rule'. All that this rule says is, that from low water, the range (conveniently still in feet on many charts) increases at a rate of 1/12th of the total range in the first hour, 2/12ths in the second hour, 3/12ths in the third hour and again in the fourth hour, after which it decreases to 2/12ths and 1/12th in the fifth and sixth hours to slack water at high water. It then repeats itself downwards again in the same ratio towards low water. I am sure that even those as mathematically inept as I am, can see that 1/12th + 2/12ths + 3/12ths + 3/12ths + 2/12ths + 1/12th = 12/12ths = 1. O.K.? Right then, let's see how it works in practise. Imagine that you are skipper of a yacht drawing 2 fathoms, i.e. 12 feet from water line to bottom of keel, and that you want to enter Blogstown-on-Sea. You look at your chart and note that there is obviously a sandbar in the entrance and only one fathom is shown at the entrance although it gets deeper further in. Your chart looks something like this:–

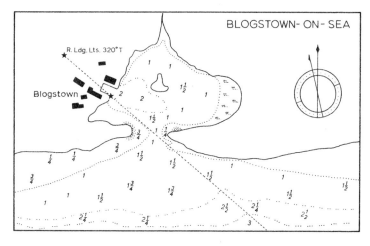

Fig. 8

You next turn to your tide tables for the correct place, date and time.

JULY						
	DATE	HIGH	RANGE		HIGH	RANGE
Tu	1	1141	5.8	.	—	—
W	2	0002	5.7	.	1220	5.1
Th	3	0047	5.4	.	1311	4.7
F	4	0153	4.7	.	1427	4.8
Sa	5	0324	4.4	.	1558	5.1
Su	6	0502	4.6	.	1720	5.5
M	7	0616	5.1	.	1833	6.0
Tu	8	0721	6.0	.	1935	6.3
W	9	0810	6.3	.	2025	6.4
Th	10	0852	6.7	.	2102	etc.
F	11	0925	6.9	.	2132	
Sa	12	0952	6.9	.	2159	
Su	13	1018	6.5	.	etc.	
M	14	1043	6.2	.		
Tu	15	1107	5.7	.		
W	16	1128	5.2	.		
Th	17	1149	4.8	.		
F	18	0001	etc.			
Sa	19	0043				
Su	19	etc.				
M	21					
Tu						

BLOGSTOWN-ON-SEA.

Fig. 9 Tide Tables of 'Blogstown-on-Sea'

Say the date is Tuesday, 8th July, the high is 0721 in the forenoon and 1935 in the afternoon, and the range at that date and time is 6 feet exactly.

These tables do not give low water, so add $6\frac{1}{4}$ hours (or halve the difference between the highs, which is only a couple of minutes different) and remembering that the spring tides are only a couple of days away on Friday and Saturday, when the range is maximum of 6 foot 9 inches, you had better play it according to the book and be sure and not sorry. Your first calculation is to add $6\frac{1}{4}$ (or 0615 hours) to the High Water time of 0721 hours:–

> 0721
> 0615
> ———
> 1336 = low water
> ———

So then, herewith your permutations of times of getting over that 6 foot sandbar:–

At 1336 (low water) you have 6 foot (chart datum), i.e. 1 fathom at the harbour entrance.

at 1436 you will have 6 foot + (1/12 of 6 foot range) = 6 foot + 6 inches = *6 foot 6 inches*

at 1536 you will have 6 foot 6 inches + (2/12 of 6 foot range) = 6 foot 6 inches + 1 foot = *7 foot 6 inches*

at 1636 you will have 7 foot 6 inches + (3/12 of 6 foot range) = 7 foot 6 inches + 1 foot 6 inches = *9 foot*

at 1736 you will have 9 foot + (3/12 of 6 foot range) = 9 foot + 1 foot 6 inches = *10 foot 6 inches*

at 1836 you will have 10 foot 6 inches + (2/12 of 6 foot range) = 10 foot 6 inches + 1 foot = *11 foot 6 inches*

at 1936 you will have 11 foot 6 inches + (1/12 of 6 foot range) = 11 foot 6 inches + 6 inches = *12 foot* which is two fathoms of water covering the bar at the harbour entrance.

So there you see the timed extent of your 6 foot range and if your yacht draws 12 feet you will just scrape the bottom if there are no waves. If you only draw 7 foot 6 inches on the other hand, you could get in any time after 1536, a little earlier if the wind is blowing the water on-shore, but you would be wise to wait with an off-shore breeze.

The strength and direction of the wind can give you quite a difference in water depth as it is pushed in or out, and you must remember that if you are looking for an anchorage because of bad weather, which is, say, a Force 7 (Near Gale) the average wave height from trough to crest could be over 12 feet, and you will be bouncing up and down with it, unless the water flattens out, as it often does, on meeting the shallows.

You must also bear in mind that with worsening weather, your barometer drops, therefore your water level will be about 1 foot lower for each 1 inch of mercury, or 37 millibars below normal, and this might be even more marked in restricted bays or estuaries.

Never forget that in seamanship, like so much else, you cannot beat the system, so if you can't beat 'em join 'em in other words, always plan your trips as far ahead as humanly possible, even if you have to make three or more alternatives, depending on weather and other unknowns, but try to work the tides getting the water to carry you the way *you* want to go. Also, apart from being quicker and easier on both you and your boat (and cheaper if powered) ideally you time your trip so that you moor or anchor at slack water and save a lot of energy, and possibly paintwork and temper too.

THREE

National Ensigns and the International Code of Signal Flags

In both your work and your hobby, it is often very difficult to decide what it would be *nice* to know and what you *must* know.

Before you cast off, whether your craft be a canoe, a pulling or rowing boat, a sailing dinghy or a motor yacht, there are half-a-dozen or so essential signals which you must know and are enlarged and explained here or elsewhere in the book, and are marked with an asterisk in the complete list at the end of this book, and the more of them you can recognise the better for you and anyone else you meet at sea.

You will note that these sketches of signal flags are shaded and not coloured. This is done for eminently practical reasons, although you might possibly find the lack of colour a little more difficult at first. At the end of the book you will see firstly that they are in plain black and white, but if you study them in greater detail, you will see that with the exception of one pair only, the *shape* of the black and the white on each flag is different. To explain more fully what I am getting at, salt water can bleach a portion of yellow on a flag to make it almost indistinguishable from a dirty white. The only two other colours used, apart from black, are red and blue, and as you can probably imagine, if they have been carried aboard let's say, a collier or a cement carrier for years, particularly if flown abaft (behind) funnels which are producing smoke from engines that are in anything but their pristine youth, you would find that from a distance the red, blue and black would all appear to be a uniform dark purple-grey. Many people do not even realize that they *are* colour-blind–even to a small extent on one colour or another–but they can still learn signal flags if they use this method of recognition.

For example, looking at the list of signal flags again, you will see that 'M' Mike is light diagonals on a dark flag, whereas 'V' Victor is dark diagonals on a light flag. The colour of Mike is white on blue, and Victor is red on white, but this doesn't matter as there are no other signal flags in the International Code with two diagonal stripes. Still referring to colours, they do not show degrees of danger like the red and green stop and go lights on the road; for example 'J' Juliett sounds one to avoid because it means 'Keep well clear of me as I have a dangerous cargo on fire'–but the flag itself is a pretty inoccuous looking blue white and blue.

The only pair which do not fit this system are Hotel (white hoist/red fly) and Kilo (yellow hoist/blue fly) but the context of these two will be made pretty clear to you anyway, firstly because Hotel (I have a pilot on board) will be flown in an 'inferior' position–that is explained shortly–and Kilo (I wish to communicate with you) in a 'superior'. There might also be four or five blasts on her hooter to attract your attention or she will be signalling by Morse to you. X-ray seems to say almost the same thing–'Stop carrying out your intentions and await my signals' but has that quite indefinable air of command of a service craft, by which I mean R.N., H.M.C.G., H.M. Customs and Excise (Waterguard), harbour masters or river authority police launches. Having myself been stopped and searched at dead of night by one of the latter half-way up the Thames, I can assure you that if you cannot separate them you are not colour blind, you are as blind as a bat and either tactless or stupid with it! That's the difference between Kilo and X-ray.

H.M. ships communicating with each other have special flags, and fishery protection ships have particular methods of shepherding and passing messages to their flock of fishing boats in cases of emergency. Some signal flags flown by an RN ship might look rather like some of those out of the International Code, but they should be ignored unless the 'code and answer' pennant

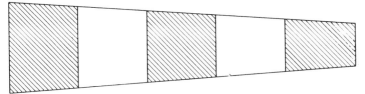

Code & answer pennant

Fig. 10

(Fig. 10) is flown which means either that her flags will be in the International Code or as an acknowledgement of a signal to her.

Purely as a matter of courtesy it will be appreciated if your vessel does not in any way interfere with a Royal Navy church service, which may well take place on deck, and while actually in progress you will notice the distinctive 'church pennant' hoisted at her yard-arm, (Fig. 11).

When referring to signal letters, you will have noticed that I have generally referred to them by a particular phonetic word. These sounds and the meanings that the *single* flags represent were altered and finally agreed by the Intergovernmental Maritime Consultative Organization (IMCO) on 1st April 1969, and are now accepted and understood by seamen who are speakers of English, French, German, Greek, Italian, Japanese, Norwegian, Russian and Spanish.

Some of the phonetic words used would appear to be odd choices, as for example 'N' Nuts might seem a lot simpler than the correct 'N' November but linguistic experts laid down their rulings

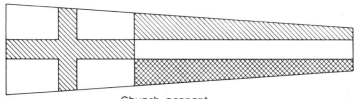

Church pennant

Fig. 11

after careful thought. Due consideration was given to the difficulty that a Russian, Japanese or a Greek might have with a particular word which is easily pronounced by a Northwest European or North American, and *vice versa*; also of course, particularly on voice radio with bad reception, the letters should not be mistaken one for another as their sound and the syllable length alters. The accentuated syllable is important to prevent errors and I have underlined the accent in the list. Most are the same but a few are not, as for example Juli*ett*, whereas many of us would pronounce it *Juli*ett. The chief use of the International Phonetic alphabet is of course on voice radio, or R/T both at sea and in the air and it is just as well to get into the hang of the system ready for the time when you achieve a radio in your boat for the first time and will have to take a simple examination by the G.P.O. on your fitness to handle the radio transmitter, but this is discussed later under Radio. So next time you have to spell out your name or a telephone exchange to a telephone operator, *use the international code*; I'm willing to take bets that most G.P.O. operators don't know the system they have helped to make international law. (Neither is it shown in most directories or phone boxes likely to be used by foreigners).

NATIONAL FLAGS AND MARITIME ENSIGNS

Seniority obviously decrees that we deal with our national flag first, and while it might seem an oddity, it is nevertheless true that the Union Flag is *never* worn by a private vessel at sea. Correctly speaking the Union Flag should only be referred to as the 'Jack' when worn at the jack-staff, i.e. the short mast right up at the sharp end of H.M. ships and was placed there in olden days where all the crew could see it, and one could be forgiven for thinking that its purpose was to remind the English, Welsh, Scots, Irish and any other nationality in the ship's company that they were fighting against the ship they were heading for and not each other. Actually though, it derives from the times when, at long range, men-of-war looked much like merchantmen, and it was in the interests of both to avoid what could be politically embarrassing mistakes by other nations.

Today, it is worn by H. M. ships in harbour only, and on few other very special occasions. Incidentally, again to use correct phraseology, vessels generally *wear* an ensign, but *fly* a flag. There is another meaning to 'fly' because it is the half of a flag flapping away from the mast, whereas the hoist is the inner portion which hoists the flag and keeps it against the mast.

One of the few instances when the Union Flag is worn at sea at the head of the mast is when the Queen is aboard H. M. Royal Yacht and, looking from stem to stern, the ship wears the Union *Jack* at her jack-staff, the Lord High Admiral's Flag (horizontal gold anchor on maroon background) at her foremast, the Royal Standard at the main, the Union *Flag* at her mizzen and the White Ensign at her ensign staff at the taffrail aft. Quite an impressive sight she makes too.

Apart from the foregoing, the Union Flag or British Ensigns Blue and Red may be worn 'defaced', as it is termed, by the addition of the badge or symbol of certain government agencies and officials and by colonial governors.

The way in which British nationality is shown at sea is by the White, Blue or Red Ensigns. The first English national ensign was worn over 400 years ago, and had a St George's cross in the top hoist and had stripes, badges or other markings in the fly, denoting the ship's port of origin.

In the early seventeenth century, the Royal Navy was divided into Red, White and Blue Fleets, each with an Admiral who was known as 'Admiral of the Blue' or 'of the White', but in 1864 the Red Ensign, or the 'Red Duster' became the official ensign of all British Merchant Ships and pleasure vessels, and has been known–loved, respected, envied, or hated –by the inhabitants of every coastline in the world for nearly 300 years.

The White Ensign is worn by H.M. Ships and R.N. Shore Establishments, and only otherwise on cenotaphs and other memorials to Royal Navy personnel. It has also been the honoured and distinguished symbol of membership of the Royal Yacht Squadron since 1859.

The defaced Blue Ensign is the National Flag of several

Commonwealth countries, but its use, either plain or defaced, anywhere at any time has very complicated requirements which are laid down by the Ministry of Defence (Navy) and contravention is a very serious offence with very severe legal implications and penalties. Plain and undefaced it is also worn by H.M. Fleet Auxilary vessels and those which consist chiefly of R.N. supply ships and tankers have a yellow anchor in the fly.

So then, we are talking basically of the Red Ensign which you can wear at all times at sea, and are strongly advised to do outside British territorial waters. In harbour it is worn during the hours of daylight only and should be hoisted as soon as you get aboard in daylight, and lowered at sunset. To be strictly correct you should lower at the signal either of the senior H.M. ship in port, or the yacht club or coastguard or harbour master. If you have died during the night the next man aboard hoists your Ensign to the peak, then lowers it to half-mast. If you don't like the way he does if you should be able to produce a clap of thunder!

By the Merchant Shipping Acts, vessels over fifty tons gross *must* wear their ensigns when entering or leaving a British port, and *all* vessels must also when entering or leaving a *foreign* port. When entering a foreign port, you must also fly the 'Yellow Jack' as it is sometimes known, but correctly is 'Q' in Quebec, plus the 'courtesy ensign' of the country you are visiting.

The 'Q' means technically, 'My ship is healthy and I require Free Pratique' (meaning from the old French, 'Your permission to carry on trade') but is nowadays taken as the signal to customs and health authorities that you have arrived from another country, even though you have only sailed, for example, less than twenty miles from Zeebrugge to Flushing. You are not normally allowed ashore until you have been cleared either by being directed to a special customs quay, or sometimes you are boarded by the customs launch. The customs officers at larger ports, well accustomed to visiting small foreign boats, such as at Cherbourg and le Havre, wait alongside the visitors' jetty of the yacht club and will come aboard once you have berthed, so you head straight for the yacht club (to whom you will have previously written warning of your arrival).

If you land at a small port where there is no resident customs officer, I would advise you firstly to report your presence to the local police. Then if you have completed the Form CG66 (and if you haven't I think you are verging on the very foolish) and you arrive at a port you did not intend to call at *please* either telephone your agent or ring the local coastguard and ask him to pass the message of your safe arrival to the H.M. Coastguard Station holding your CG66. All this is most important as you will gather more fully in the chapter on search and rescue services.

The courtesy ensign is the national maritime flag of the country you are visiting, and must be smaller than your own ensign, and foreign vessels in British ports reciprocate by wearing the Red Ensign. You might occasionally see the Union Flag worn as a courtesy ensign but this is incorrect.

The next question generally asked is 'Where do I hang all this lot at the same time?' The answer is complicated by the type of boat you have but is based on the importance allotted to each flag which decides its position in your boat (or the importance of each part of your boat deciding the position of the flag – choose yourself).

The 'Senior' priority position is at the stern, i.e. from the quarter-deck or poop of the ships of old which was the captain's and officers' domain, and from where the ship was directed. The next senior is the starboard yard arm, followed by the port yard. Ideally then, you should enter a foreign port with your ensign at the ensign-staff right aft, the smaller courtesy ensign at the starboard yardarm and 'Q' Quebec at your port yardarm. *Never* should any of the three be flown from your mast head (although you can have a small triangular pennant representing your yacht club, the R.N.L.I., if you are a member, or any small piece of light bunting (to show you down there what the wind is doing up there).

If the sail-boom of your yacht swings too low and near to your stern or transom to have your ensign staff shipped there while actually sailing (that is, not under power) you should either wear your ensign at the gaff or if Bermudian rigged, the ensign is worn two-thirds the way up the leech (*qv*), but to repeat, these are only permissible positions if the ensign staff cannot be shipped in its correct position aft.

If you are in a motor boat of the type with no appreciable mast, and you intend being out at night, off-shore, or 'going foreign' I would suggest you seriously consider and take professional advice on the advantages of a mast even with no permanent sail attached. Firstly, if your motor or screw fails, you can rig a sail from a sleeping bag or blanket and get yourself to shore, secondly if you are in trouble you can communicate with flags by day or Morse from your mast head light at night, and when fog comes down, it is remarkably comforting to have a radar reflector aloft.

INTERNATIONAL CODE OF SIGNAL FLAGS

Coming now to signal flags, one that you will frequently see is the pilot flag. Pilots are all licensed most by Trinity House which governs London district and many outports, but there are other pilotage authorities, and the Pilotage Act of 1913 lays down quite strict financial penalties if the incoming vessel refuses or defaults in supplying correct details of tonnage and cargo when asking for a pilot's services. H.M. ships and registered fishing vessels are exempt from pilotage dues, as are pleasure yachts under fifty tons gross who are not carrying fee-paying passengers, saleable goods or cargo. On the next two pages are some of the flags you must know in order that you treat their wearers with the respect they deserve and keep well out of their way because when you cast off in harbour in your new boat for the very first time you could well risk your boat–or your own life.

Just as a reminder and to save you flipping the pages back to the beginning the colours are denoted by:–

White   Yellow   Red   Blue   Black

Fig. 12

I am keeping to the same principle that yellow is a slightly darkened white, and blue often appears darker than red. Black and white will, I trust, be obvious, otherwise you really *are* colour blind and I would not set out to sea at all if I were you.

There are three flags concerned with pilotage, the first being the pilot flag itself which distinguishes the pilot's boat, and the word 'pilot' is usually in white on the pilot boat's side. Reminder: 'It's ice-cool on deck but red-hot in the engine-room.'

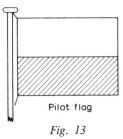

Pilot flag

Fig. 13

Same colours as 'Pilot' but sideways = 'H' Hotel = 'I have a pilot on board.' Often cross-channel ferries have locally qualified officers with a licence, which might also be granted to some local fisherman. Main ports of course have full-time professionals and for a big ship, some doing just a small or intricate passage (i.e. Thames, Mersey or Severn amongst a few). These are usually on stand-by rota by day and night. The associated flag is 'G' Golf = 'I require a Pilot.' The signal can be given by flag, morse, light or horn, or of course, radio-telephone.

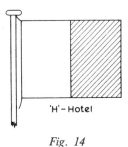

'H' – Hotel

Fig. 14

'B' Bravo (sometimes with white circle in centre meaning petroleum spirit) shows she is handling highly inflammable or explosive products. Do not berth alongside, and on behalf of your insurance agent, may I ask you not to stub your fag end out on her in passing!

There are three flags which show a ship's *intended* future movement, often flown

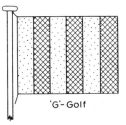

'G'– Golf

Fig. 15

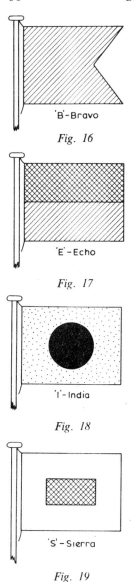

'B'-Bravo

Fig. 16

'E'-Echo

Fig. 17

'I'-India

Fig. 18

'S'-Sierra

Fig. 19

in harbour. The movement may take some time to take effect and you have to judge whether you can pass in safety or whether to heave-to and wait. Of course she will turn more rapidly if unladen, and beware of her screws which might be partly out of the water, but look at her Plimsoll mark (*qv*) or water line for the clues.

The three flags (*Figs. 17–19*) are 'E' Echo = to starboard; 'I' India = to Port; 'S' Sierra = operating astern propulsion. These will usually be reinforced by one, two or three short blasts on her horn being, as you will see from the table at the end, 'E', 'I' and 'S' in Morse, i.e. . . . and . . . Four or five blasts is general warning to all shipping to keep clear (or just wake up!).

If, out at sea, you see two fishing boats each flying a flag which looks rather like the French national flag, except that it is red, white and blue (whereas the French is blue, white and red) it is 'T' Tango which means 'I am engaged in pair trawling', meaning that they each have one end of a very long net that they are pulling through the water between them. Therefore, for the sake of harmony amongst the professional and amateur boating fraternity, the health of your bank balance and keeping the air free from verbal pollution, do not sail between the two because you will almost certainly cut or snarl up their net which will make both of you rather cross, and you will be in the wrong. Were you to do this very foolish thing, you would probably be told facts about your antecedents which might shock or even distress and amaze you.

There are only two more flags to learn in this chapter, and they are such that you might well be extremely glad if someone else flew them on your behalf one day, although I hope it is never necessary. The first is 'O' Oscar = man overboard. At this signal all seamen, whatever they are doing at the time, leave it and help in the search, because it is extremely difficult to see a man in the water even a hundred yards away, particularly if there are a few waves and surfing rollers. He might have his face away from you and, if swimming, you won't see his arms, and he may present only a tiny dark blob against a dark background.

The other signal is 'Y' Yankee, which means 'I am dragging my anchor'. Even though you might only have a small boat, your help might be just enough to save the boat—or even a life as it means that his anchor is slipping (through mud, weed, light sand or kelp) and his power cannot get him off a lee-shore.

Flags are of little practical use unless a minimum size of 24 inches × 30 inches (about 70 centimetres × 85 centimetres) so remember that if you intend to register your boat (*qv*) you will need signal halliards high enough to take the

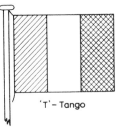

'T' – Tango

Fig. 20

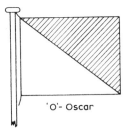

'O' – Oscar

Fig. 21

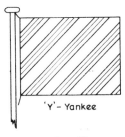

'Y' – Yankee

Fig. 22

hoist of your code number. You will find this much easier when identifying yourself to someone than having to send the eighteen flags that would be necessary if your boat's name were, say *Caernarvon Castle IV*!

The flags I would recommend you to carry–apart from your ensign of course–are:–

Q – I have just arrived from another country
U – You are running into danger
V – Please assist me
Y – My anchor is not holding
F – I am disabled
O – Man overboard

Plus –The courtesy ensigns of any countries you might visit, even by accident or storm, so if you are visiting a mid-channel port in Belgium, for example, while you are about it buy a French and a Dutch ensign at the same time in case you are blown off course.

Although I have referred earlier to the fact that the R.N. flies the 'code and answer pennant' to show that she is using the International Code of Signals, there are at least three flags which she might fly in harbour without the pennant, and which might be of interest to you.

'Q' Quebec, normally meaning having arrived from abroad, means that she wishes to recall any or all of her boats. If it be an exercise you'll see quite a race.

Another to watch carefully as always is 'U' Uniform, which really still means 'You are running into danger' if you are near, as it means that she is working cable, that is that she might be securing to a buoy or mooring, or re-deploying an anchor, and in most of these cases will have boats with either heavy chain or cable aboard, or even an anchor slung under one boat or lashed between two. In all events, keep clear.

The last is our 'V' Victor, red diagonals on a white flag (I am in need of assistance). If you, all breezy, helpful and matey-like were to sail your 14-foot dinghy up to say, H.M.S. *Ark Royal*, and ask if you can help, the laughter would ring like Westminster Chimes all around the country, because the Royal Navy hoists that flag to show that she is now open and prepared to receive visitors.

Your ears would burn red for the rest of your natural life–and as there are bound to be at least a few seamen in Heaven–probably longer.

FOUR

Lights and Buoys

Although they could well warrant at least one chapter each, I have made lights and buoys into two sections of one chapter from which you should gain the rudiments of the systems, at least.

Lights are particularly important, and the need for instant recognition of the only thing you can see on a pitch-black night must be obvious, and you can only hope that the *other* skipper sees you and is also sailing appropriately lighted.

The code of correct lights at sea is laid down by British Merchant Shipping Acts, and forms a very important part of the *International Rules for Preventing Collisions at Sea* (1972) and already has embraced quite a lot more major amendments, and is probably continuing to do so while this book is being run off the presses, so you can imagine the constant necessity of keeping up to date with current and international legislation as more nations come into the E.E.C., or become members of I.M.C.O.

If any damage is caused by your contravention of these regulations, then very expensive legal liabilities could follow, and, note, even unintentional contravention is liable because, as usual, ignorance of the law is not an excuse.

Apart from the purely legal aspect though, correct lights are even more vital at sea than they are on the roads, because they can tell you (if you know how) quite a lot about the type and size of the other ship, her rough course and speed, and also her intentions if she is doing something which could affect or damage you.

All vessels. regardless of size, must carry lights between the hours of sunset and sunrise when under way, or if anchored or moored in a sea-way.

Various combinations of red, white and green are the colours normally used, blue seldom, and orange is usually reserved either as a marker for the search and rescue services in an emergency, and sometimes orange stain is used to assist in the study of tidal and current flow.

Before going more deeply into the subject, one small but important point to note is your cabin decor. The reason for this will be obvious when you remember that left-hand = port = red (same colour as the wine), and right-hand = starboard = green, (both looking forward towards the sharp end). If you have *green* curtains with your cabin lights showing through the port-holes (or scuttles) on the *port* side, someone is entitled to think that you are travelling in the opposite direction, and the hitherto peaceful confines of your cabin might well be broken in more ways than one by the sharp end of a rapidly moving vessel in the process of cutting your beloved boat in two. A most unpleasant thought, but one well worth keeping in mind.

A small dinghy is allowed legally to get away without fixed lights, but only provided there is a torch or lighted lantern that can be exhibited in sufficient time to prevent a collision. It is a better practise though, and a lot safer, to have a 'combination light,' which can be quite small enough to be readily portable, and consists of a lantern-type battery, and red and green coloured side panels, and the whole thing can be either held aloft or hitched to the spare oar (which a dinghy should always carry), or to the boat-hook.

As the regulations are very specific over the details of lights, I think it better to quote sections of the relevant rules; anyone checking on the accuracy will notice that I have telescoped some rules that are repeated, and that I have not—and do not intend to—quote the several long paragraphs which startles you into a state approaching ecstatic rapture with the revelation that 'vessels shall be deemed to be sight of one another only when one can be observed visually from the other' (Rule 3k). I am sure that that has

cleared a lot of fog from your mind (or has it made it worse?).
Anyway, I will 'translate' the regulations leaving out or including
the references to other paragraphs or rules, and give you the bare
facts.

Lights for Small Vessels

Power-driven vessels of 65 feet in length, vessels under oars or
sails of less than 40 feet in length, when under way, shall be
provided with the following lights:–

(i) Where it can best be seen and not less than three feet above
the side-lights, a white light visible all around through 360
degrees for a distance of not less than two miles.

Note: The visibility referred to assumes a clear night with good
visibility, i.e. no mist or fog.

(ii) On the appropriate sides shall be shown a green and a red
light showing an unbroken arc of light from right ahead to $112\frac{1}{2}$
degrees (10 points of the compass when referred to by the now
rather out-moded 32 point compass card). These lights should
be visible at a distance of at least one mile, and so fixed that the
green and red sidelights shall have inboard screens projecting at
least 3 feet forward of the lights, so as to prevent these lights
from being seen across the bows.

Well, I trust that that is quite sufficient to enable you to make
your boat legal–and what is more important–visible at sea. It is
rather complicated, and if your boat is of such a shape as to make it
awkward, a visit to a boat-yard, or show a sketch to H.M.
Coastguard or your harbour master, and you will no doubt be
given some ideas of how to comply with the rules.

Let's consider the two extremes of a dinghy and an ocean
liner. I've explained the side or navigation lights, and the stern
light which for a small boat is one all-round light. When you
consider a large ship, on the other hand, you will appreciate that
between the fo'c'sle head and the after-deck, i.e. the sharp end and
the blunt end, of a ship over 150 feet in length, there is a
considerable amount of traditional ironmongery such as the

bridge, radio cabin and chart-room, but also life-boats and their supporting davits, masts about the girth of a medium-sized oaktree, their supporting wire-work, plus radio aerials and antennae long and short, signal halliards thick and thin, and radar scanners of all conceivable shapes and sizes. The combination light referred to earlier would be quite useless under these circumstances, so to give the observer an idea of size of ship he is about to meet, the Rules specify differences for vessels under 40 feet in length, 40 feet–65 feet, 65 feet–150 feet, and those over 150 feet in length.

To give you a rough idea of the lengths we are considering, one seldom finds two masts on a vessel under 30 foot LOA (length over-all), a typical North Sea trawler would be about 250 g.t. (gross tonnage), and about 120 feet long, a 1500 ton R.N. frigate about 350 feet, and the best-known Atlantic liners approaching 1000 feet and over 50,000 gross tons. Nowadays, of course, even they would be dwarfed by the giant oil-tankers where one talks of lengths of a quarter-mile or more.

However, the basic rule for the lights of vessels under way remains the same (with the exceptions made for *some* fishing vessels and sailing vessels not under power), that navigation lights should be shown on their proper sides only, and an all-round white light appreciably above them.

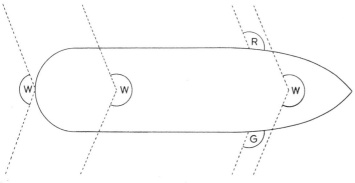

Fig. 23 Lights on a Large Ship

Perhaps Fig. 23 will explain the rules better than words.

Note that in addition to these rules, there is a proviso that to make her identity perfectly clear, a sailing vessel not propelled by any means except the wind must carry side lights (or navigation lights), and an 'overtaking light', but not the white masthead light denoting a powered craft. She may, if she so wishes, additionally carry a red light over green at the top of her foremast. This, of course, is purely to point out to powered craft that she is at the mercy of the winds, and therefore would be pleased if you would give way to her.

If, therefore, you see only a *single* green or red light plus a white mast-head light, you have three questions you must immediately ask yourself–and come up with the correct answer pretty darned quick–and be correct ...

(1) This vessel could be crossing my bows, could there be a collision?

(2) If it looks that a collision is possible, should she give way, or shall I?

(3) Are we both on parallel courses and without danger to each other?

I say (quite intentionally) several times in this book 'Danger in sight–turn right', but if there be the slightest doubt in your mind, play for safety and give a touch of Starboard wheel, (telling your navigator of your change of course, and again when you have regained your original bearing when danger is passed). It is surprising, but a small change of course, if not plotted on the chart could make quite an appreciable difference at the end of the day. If you are sailing alone, you should always have a pad at hand anyway, so jot down time off course.

It is impossible to describe fully all the permutations of lights you could see, so you will have to learn to do the necessary mental cross-word puzzles rapidly, and the next few pages show you a few for you to try.

Remember that most of these examples are taken as looking dead ahead or on your beam, but they will look very different when either you or the other vessel are on converging or diverging courses, particularly when at acute angles.

Here are fourteen examples of the easier sort for you to try out, and to give you an idea of how the Rules work in practise.

Do not forget the old, old story about the crack-shot sahib who fired dead between the eyes, but missed as he had fired between two one-eyed tigers. In other words, if you see a green and a red light, do not automatically assume that both lights are carried by the same vessel. Confusing isn't it?

The most difficult of that little lot, I personally find, is the fishing vessels. So who do you turn to for assistance before setting out at night but your ever-ready friend and ally against the sea, H.M. Coastguard. He will know from his vast storehouse of local knowledge that with this wind and that weather and a particular time of year you might find trawlers on their way up north, drifters moving almost imperceptibly with the tide, the locals out for mackerel, and the lobster-pots just around a certain point. If you approach the coastguard, as I once did, in waters I did not know, you will be met with absolutely invariable punctilious courtesy as I was—even more so if you say frankly 'I don't know about this area. What do you think I should do, or who should I see?' There is no sense in ignoring a man who is paid and trained to know your troubles. On this occasion, the Coastguard told me to take it very steady for at least the first ten miles, as he said 'There'll be —— idiots floating broadside with no anchor, some with no lights, others with lights the wrong way round.' It was a grand fishing match, and as he pointed out whether the blind incomprehension, or the intrepidity of some boats fishing away as if for gold was anything to go by, they caused a hazard and could cause a casualty, but there was nothing he could do about it apart from hoping and having sublime faith in the survival of a fool.

This is, I must admit, an isolated incident, but when I sailed out, things were exactly as he said. If I had sailed out at fifteen knots or more, I could have killed up to twelve people on the very first boat that loomed up out of the darkness with no lights whatever.

However, whilst on the subject of fishermen, it will help you to know the three basic definitions of fishermen, and how their fishing could affect you.

D

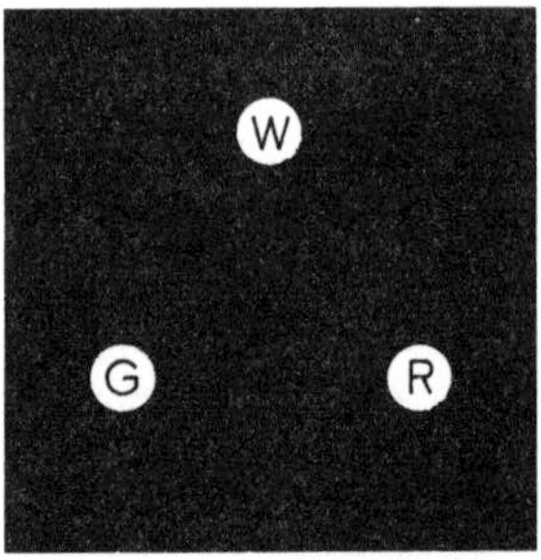

Fig. 24
POWER VESSEL LESS THAN 150
FEET   LONG   HEADING
STRAIGHT AT YOU.

Fig. 25
SAILING   VESSEL   HEADED
STRAIGHT   TOWARDS   YOU,
BUT   CARRYING   HER
(OPTIONAL) MAST LIGHTS.

Fig. 26
POWER VESSEL LESS THAN 150
FEET LONG CROSSING YOUR
BOWS LEFT-RIGHT.

Fig. 27
POWER VESSEL *OVER* 150 FEET
CROSSING YOUR BOWS LEFT-
RIGHT.
N.B. The *lower* light is always the
for'ard end, the higher white light
towards the stern.

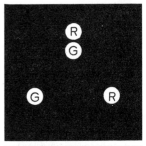

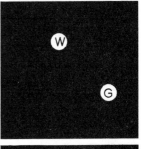

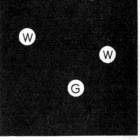

Fig. 28
A POWER TOWING VESSEL SHOWS HER OWN WHITE MASTLIGHT PLUS ONE FOR EACH VESSEL TOWED, (length of tow under 600 feet. When over, an extra light is carried.
THIS VESSEL IS TOWING TWO OTHERS, THE TOTAL LENGTH IS UNDER 600 FEET AND THE REAR BARGE AN OVERTAKING LIGHT, AND IS CROSSING YOUR BOWS LEFT-RIGHT.

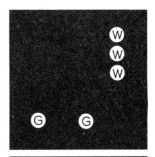

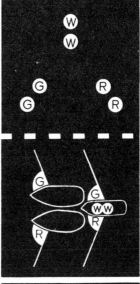

Fig. 29
A TUG COMING TOWARDS YOU IS *PUSHING* TWO BARGES.
(The first time you see this you feel like signing the Temperance Pledge)

THE SAME THING, BUT VIEWED FROM ABOVE AS IT IS RATHER CONFUSING. NOTE THE WIDTH OF THE BARGES.
AS THE LENGTH IS ONLY FOR ONE, SHE CARRIES TWO MASTHEAD LIGHTS ONLY.

Fig. 30
VESSEL NOT UNDER COMMAND (i.e. she cannot manoeuvre freely for some reason or another), BUT STOPPED IN THE WATER. IF MAKING WAY (SAY, WITH DODGY STEERING GEAR, SHE WOULD CARRY TWO RED MASTHEAD LIGHTS WITH NORMAL NAVIGATION LIGHTS.)

Fig. 31
FISHING VESSELS, ALWAYS
DIFFICULT TO IDENTIFY. N.B.
UNLIKE Fig. 52, THERE ARE NO
NAVIGATION LIGHTS *IF NOT
UNDER WAY.*
THIS HAS GEAR EXTENDING
500 FEET OR LESS, AND WILL
SHOW ONLY HER LOWER
WHITE LIGHT *WHEN
APPROACHED* BY ANOTHER
VESSEL.

Fig. 32
FISHING BOAT AT ANCHOR
WITH GEAR OF 500 FEET OR
LESS EXTENDED IN THE
DIRECTION OF THE LOWER
LIGHT. (Note: difference is marginal,
but could be crucial if you *have* to pass
close by her.)

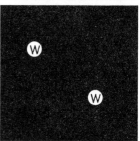
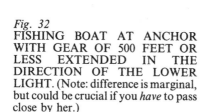

Fig. 33
HERE IS A *TRAWLER*
STEAMING TOWARDS YOU
TOWING HER NETS ASTERN, SO
YOU MUST KEEP WELL CLEAR
TO BOTH SIDES OF HER.

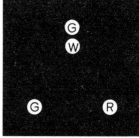
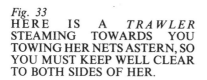

Fig. 34
TWO TRAWLERS TOWING AND
SUPPORTING ENDS OF A NET
*SO YOU MUST NOT SAIL
BETWEEN THEM.*
N.B. Although there is not a war in
European waters at the moment, there
are still mine-sweepers and they carry
the same lights.

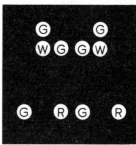

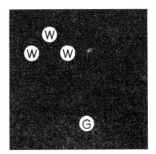

Fig. 35
VERY DISTINCTIVE – FISHING
VESSEL UNDER WAY AND
WITH LINES OR NETS
*EXTENDING MORE THAN 500
FEET.*
AS THIS ONE CANNOT FREELY
MANOEUVRE YOU OBVIOUSLY
TREAT HER WITH THE
GREATEST OF CAUTION.

Fig. 36
A PILOT VESSEL (Rule 8) – An easy
way to remember 'It's OK on deck but
red-hot in the engine room'.
CARRIES SIDE AND STERN
LIGHTS WHEN UNDER WAY (an
additional light and flare when at
anchor–seldom seen–see chapter on
S.A.R.)

Fig. 37

THE MOST DIFFICULT OF ALL
TO IDENTIFY:
1. You are overtaking a vessel,
2. A small boat,
3. A lamp-post on shore (I've been
    had on that one)
4. A vessel up to 150 feet anchored
    in a sea-way,
5. A fishing vessel that has not
    spotted your approach,
6. A bright star or planet generally
    at sunset or sunrise,
7. A fisherman examining lobster-
    or crab-pots (or looking for them
    with a spot-light.)
8. A ship in the distance where you
    have seen her masthead light, but
    not yet her navigation lights.

As we are concerned with the coastal waters of the U.K. only, in this book, you must remember that whilst there might be a closed season for catching one breed of fish, just as there is for game-birds, in our case the technique of fishing can be changed and another family of fish with different breeding or feeding habits can be caught. In other words, on every day of the year there are fish of one sort or another to be caught around our shores. All these fish might not be accepted with the traditional chips, and they might not all have the romantic (but often wrongly used) names of sea-trout, or sea-salmon. We will have to get used to the fact that our favourite fish—or those which we have acquired taste for are becoming scarcer, so we will have to learn to broaden our tastes if we wish to eat fish at all, because there are still plenty of fish, it is simply certain varieties that are scarcer.

The professionalism of our fisherman means that they know where the fish are, in which direction they are travelling and why, and finally at what depth they are. Here are the three basic methods of professional fishing:—

(A) *Trolling*

This is fishing with lines over the stern, usually for mackerel which I personally think is the finest flavoured fish in the sea (particularly if eaten within an hour or so of catching). Trolling is done at very slow speed, one or two knots only, with often one or more longish lines with half-a-dozen or more lines attached with medium sized hooks to each, and 'feathers', often 2 inch lengths of plastic tassle, or the silver lining of a cigarette packet, in short almost anything that glistens or waves. If you see a crowd of fishing boats, you will know that they have found a shoal, as you will seldom find a lone mackerel.

If you do find a shoal with other fishermen already fishing, handle your boat with the greatest of care.

Whether you wish to join in the benefits of the shoal or not, if you come too close aft of the boats you will snarl up their lines, if you cross their bows too close you might split up the shoal. In either case the invective will prove to be–at least–educational.

(B) *Trawling*

Trawlers operate in a very different way, and require even more caution on your part.

They will be dragging a vast net with floats on the top and weights on the bottom. If two of them have one end each they are pair trawling and (See chapter on flags) show appropriate signals by day or night.

They move at a steady speed and course and often pick up all their catch from mid-depth water. If ground-fishing they might come up with old mines, unexploded bombs, and other flora and fauna together with other dangerous and very inedible bits and pieces.

According to the cunning of the skipper, and, of course with intelligent use of sophisticated electronic aids, the trawl can be raised or lowered as he thinks fit.

The necessity for absolute team-work will be understood when you consider that in volcanic areas such as the Mid-Atlantic Ridge, stretching some 5000 miles from Iceland, through the Azores and to the Equator, and where the mythical city of Atlantis is reputed to be, the depth can alter from zero to 600 feet and in some places to 6000 feet deep *within one mile.*

However, assuming you will not be trawling off Iceland this summer, I trust that you will realise that he is dredging the sea-bed for our food, and the strain on his trawl-wires combined with his speed is tremendous, so if ever you see a trawler, remember that as he cannot alter speed or direction quickly, give him a wide berth.

(C) *Drifting*

This is yet another form of fishing for the man who really knows what he is doing. In this case he has a large scoop-net out astern, and as the name implies, drifts–*but with his bows into the tide stream or current*–hence the need for a good look-out to tell you which way he is moving. He lays, head into stream, and simply stops the fish as they float past. He might give a quick kick ahead with his engines to keep his head in the right direction and his lines taut, but often he has a small sail, often he uses the mizzen, which will enable him to keep his station in the water without alarming the fish. Like trawling, this is sometimes carried out by two vessels with the net between them, and they could be several hundreds of yards apart, then coming gradually closer together, closing the net as the two boats come together and they each heave the net on board and disgorge its contents.

I have deliberately gone into the fishing details in length, although in a chapter on lights and buoys, but I trust that you will now appreciate the importance of recognising the lights shown by fishermen at sea.

Particularly off the French coast, you might see green flares every ten minutes or so which, I think, are a first-rate idea, as it gives your navigator ample time to work out an avoiding course without too much waste of time on your part, and this is really what good seamanship is all about, isn't it?

NAUTICAL SIGNPOSTS

One of the more irritating or fascinating things about buoys is that they come in almost all shapes and sizes, and cover (in more ways than one) a multitude of sins.

To start with is the inconvenience of having two different types or meanings i.e. the lateral system, which has been used in this country for some hundreds of years, but there is also the cardinal system which is gradually being introduced from the Continent. To make it more annoying still, I consider myself a loyal subject of Her Majesty and imbued with the traditions of the sea with the Royal and Merchant Navies, but yet I have to admit that the cardinal system of buoys referred to is better and more fool-proof than ours. So I had better explain what each system is, otherwise, sooner or later you will not only find yourself up the creek without a paddle, but you won't know what direction to paddle in when you have found one.

THE LATERAL SYSTEM OF BUOYAGE

This means, basically, that your buoys are marked by shape or colour *according to the lateral movement of the water*. That means that you are always assumed to be looking for, or being guided by the lateral movement or flood tide, which is the ideal time to enter harbour (in theory, anyway), and it assumes that whatever the water is doing at the time, when you *come out* of that harbour, you transpose left to mean right, and *vice versa.*

Starboard-Hand Buoy is the one which should be left on your starboard or right-hand side *as you enter harbour*, I stress again. It is conical in shape, should be painted black, and on top can have just a pole, or an 'X', or a lattice-work basket. In the last case the irreverent say the basket is there to hold the sandwich lunch which the fisherman's wife has rowed out in the family dinghy to put there for him, the reverent say the basket-work dates from the days when the most holy St Something-or-other used to fight his way against often overwhelming odds of the elements, struggling in his boat, to fill the container with charcoal and peat or whatever to guide the faithful home. Like most old stories, there might be a grain of truth in it somewhere if you dig deep enough.

Starboard is the Priority side of your vessel, so if buoys are numbered, starboard buoys start with 1, then 3, 5, 7, 9, etc. If you are suddenly turning to starboard you give one single blast on your syren or hooter. The lights on the buoys are usually white and will flash 1, 3, or 5.

Port-hand buoy is the one which should be left on your port or left-hand side *as you enter harbour*. It is barrel-shaped, that is rather like a fifty gallon oil drum, and should be painted red, or sometimes in a red-and-white chequered pattern. This one seldom has the saint's fire-basket (or fisherman's lunch-box) attached. If it be numbered, the series (again from seaward) will start with 2, and continue 4, 6, 8, 10, etc. Red lights flash the same sequence.

There are several troubles with this system. the first is that, although one should always be concentrating while in charge of a boat, it is very easy to find yourself coming *out* of harbour, and, your mind being clouded with things, (Not gin, I trust) when you see a port-hand buoy, one is apt to treat it as a port-hand buoy and leave it on your port hand. But, you see, you are going against the flood, or in other words going *towards* the sea, and not coming in with it, so you reverse your training and knowledge and have to leave the port-hand buoy on your starboard side. Confusing, I think you will agree.

I remember several years ago crossing from one side of the Thames Estuary to the other, from Margate on the southern shore, to Southend on the northern, which is about the same distance as Dover to Calais. I then carried on weaving up the Thames.

I found middle-ground buoys, which are spherical, painted with horizontal stripes and have diamond-shapes on the seaward end and triangles on the up-river end, but as there were both port-hand and starboard-hand buoys marking the two channels up either (optional) side of the central sand-bank marked by the middle-ground buoys, I came to the rapid conclusion that a starboard-hand buoy tells you starboard, I agree, but starboard of what? The only answer, of course, (pun unintentional, I assure you) is what is

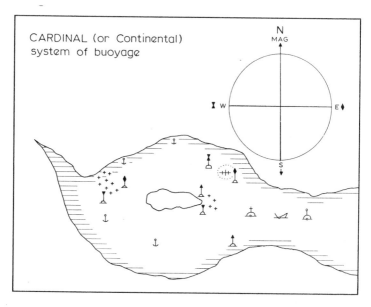

Fig. 38

your compass course on your chart? In that case, if you know where you are, you are only using the buoys as a check to ensure that you are where your compass and chart tell you you are.

The cardinal system is, in my opinion anyway, much simpler for both the amateur and the professional to follow.

Here it is in diagram form (Fig. 38):

I hope that little sketch will have helped you to understand what is a very new concept. What the buoys say or even, one might say, command, is 'you will sail to the north of me', or 'the south of me,' or to 'the east' or to 'the west.' In my little sketch below you will find what I hope will be helpful reminders of which is which, when you meet one.

BEARING	BUOY	MEANING	REMINDER
North		You should sail north of me	 To north pole
South		You should sail south of me	 To south pole
East		You should sail east of me	 'e' for east
West		You should sail west of me	 West

Fig. 39 Reminder Table for the Cardinal System of Buoyage

FIVE

Anchoring and Mooring

You will not be in your first boat for very long before you discover that there is no pedal or lever marked brake. How are you supposed to stop once you are going then? So, gentle reader (as they say in all the best books) if you have not yet read the chapter on tides, I should consider it carefully if I were you, otherwise some bits of this chapter will not make sense.

You are confronted with a fairly limited choice of methods of stopping at sea, and here is a list of your main alternatives, the theories of which do not alter basically whether you are under sail or power, but I will enlarge on each alternative later.

Assuming that you know little or nothing about the problems facing you, you can:–

(a) try to catch a buoy to hang on to, and attach a rope
(b) drop anchor
(c) come alongside a pier or quay and hope someone will be there to grab your line
(d) take refuge alongside another boat, hoping not to damage it, or worse, to ram it fair and square
(e) run aground
(f) pull out the bung, which is rather sordid, messy and generally unnecessary

Now let us examine the odds on each of these, except the last two which are explained elsewhere, and, what is most important, by doing so, try to reduce the odds of you or someone else getting hurt, and boats being damaged or sunk.

The point is that wind, tide streams and currents push your boat, and the good seaman is the one who takes advantage of this fact and deliberately allows himself to be pushed, *but in the direction in which he wants to go.*

If you try to fight wind or tide, you will seldom, if ever, win. I'm afraid that I refer to this in almost every chapter because it cannot be stressed enough that wind and water are very different from tyres and tarmac.

Here are two diagramatic sketches which show what actually happens to you under the simplest circumstances.

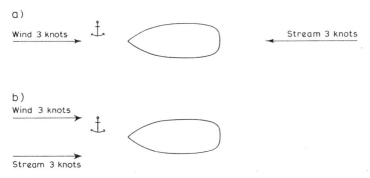

Fig. 40 Principles of Mooring considering Wind/Tide effect

You must always keep in the back of your mind that your cool, calm and unembarrassing mooring or anchoring, depends entirely on your having *previously* worked out very carefully, which way the surface wind and water will be moving you when and where you want to stop, and what effects these two forces acting on your boat will have.

If you are dead lucky, as in 'A' above, they cancel each other out, but in 'B' they double up on each other in which case you turn into it and gently allow your speed to drop to nil. But there is also a third alternative where the two forces take the 'blame and effect' between each.

I hope these two sketches help demonstrate my point:–

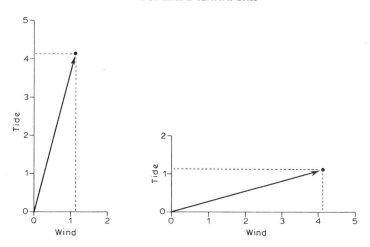

Fig. 41 Graphs of Wind/Tide Effect on your Boat

As you can see, you simply count off the estimated wind and stream speeds on any old handy bit of paper for a start, using any convenient units, but you will soon find yourself doing it automatically in your head. You count the speeds to give you your resultant course, i.e. from 'O' to 'X', and this is the line along which your boat will drift if you take no action to counteract it.

These sketches are only to give you a rough idea of what a resultant is, as the subject is covered more fully in books dealing with coastal navigation.

I have assumed that a four knot wind pushes you at four knots, which is not strictly true, and these two examples, of course, are both where the wind and stream are at rightangles, which they seldom are, but still, not to worry, it is only marginally more complicated when they are not, but it is not difficult. If I can understand it, I'm jolly sure that you can.

Well, having cleared the air a bit about the basics of the problem, take a closer look at each of the four alternatives referred to earlier.

MOORING TO BUOYS

As I advise strongly in the chapter on buoys, never secure to a navigation buoy, firstly because its moorings were not designed to take the extra sideways pull of a boat, and if you pull it off its moorings the authority may demand quite a packet from you for repairing or replacing them, and secondly, you may well be hiding the buoy from someone who is searching for it as a navigational aid, and they might sail into serious trouble. Strictly speaking the term mooring should only be used when lying to *two* anchors or buoys, one at each end. (The Moorish pirates' captives were secured hand and foot. This is the best derivation I can think of anyway. If you can think of a better one, good luck!)

Picking up a mooring single-handed is one of the trickiest of sailing manoeuvres, and even the finest seaman will admit–if forced–that he has come unstuck at some time or another, but there is a lot you can do to perfect the art and minimise the chances of an ignominious failure which always seems to occur when it appears that at least half the population of the country is watching, while your first real success always seems to be unobserved. So when you are out on the sea, and well away from everyone, secure a line to (say) a plastic bottle with a loop to it, or an old life jacket, and try coming up to it at different speeds and from different directions, because whether it be a sailing boat where you come up into the wind to stop, or a power boat where you cut your engine, no two boats—even of similar type and design seem to act in exactly the same way. As capricious as women they are!

Your first essential tool for mooring is a boat hook. There are two main types (Fig. 42 see overleaf).

Ideally of course, have one of each type aboard because you often need two because you have two ends to your boat, and because of the differing use of each. Type (A) is ideal for pushing off from a wooden quay or fending off a stout wooden boat, and although the point may make a small dent in the woodwork it is better for this purpose than type (B) which is liable to slip against a smooth, wet surface and cause a collision. The disadvantage of (A)

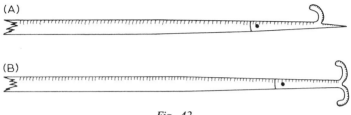

Fig. 42

is the possibility of puncturing inflatables and light plastic (particularly polystyrene 'pram' dinghies) as well as (and I have known this to happen), holing and sinking the owner's own treasured plastic mooring buoy.

Above all, if you are going to have a boat hook, for goodness' sake have a boat hook, of stout metal, double screwed securely into a sound, stout shaft–eight foot is not too long, nine foot better.

Some of the one inch by four foot broom-handles one sees with a not very glorified cup hook on the end are worse than useless, because they can let you down when you need to depend on them most. I know that eight to nine foot seems ridiculously long, but you'll find mooring simplified by having just that extra foot or so.

Anyway, there are patent types which fold or screw together, and with a little constructive thought they can be stowed flat on deck, or sometimes clipped to your mast, ready for use but not in your way while sailing. If you have more money than me, you can buy, instead of longing for, a very expensive but ingenious fibreglass and stainless steel job, with a patent hook and loop release which must be a wonderful tool for the single-handed sailor.

There are two main types of mooring buoy, one a heavy one to which you make fast through a whacking great ring, and often ribbed with battens of wood, so let's deal with that type first. Unless it is only a temporary stop-off while you cook a meal or such, do not just use rope, as the ring on the buoy will be rusty and will saw through your comparatively light line pretty quickly unless it is securely tightened around the ring. Your mooring should, in any case, have a hard eye spliced into it, and you should have a shackle all ready to fit if needed.

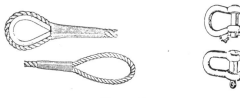

Figure 43

Ideally, if securing to a buoy for an over-night stay, you should have a three fathom length of chain cable and you simply pass this chain through the ring of the buoy and bring both ends back aboard where you secure with a shackle. Here you have the added advantage that if the wind starts to get up in the night you should be wakened by the clanking of the chains on the hollow steel buoy.

There are two further points to bear in mind here. Someone at sometime put that mooring buoy there to moor to, so to avoid an argument in the middle of the night with an irate fisherman who has been out working, and finds his 'parking space' has been nicked by a 'foreigner', I would strongly advise dropping into the port and harbour master's office to ask him if you can lie there for the night, and of course, offering to pay. If he knows that this particular buoy is being used he will direct you to another, or show you the visiting boats' moorings elsewhere or alongside the quay. Do not leave this too late–it is far better to nip in at about 1500 to 1600 hours and get it fixed, then go out to sea again for a few hours if you want to, but knowing exactly where you can get your head down for the night. Using this approach, I have never yet evinced the slightest problem, and very seldom has payment been accepted for an overnight stay, and then the payment was only pretty nominal.

Mooring alongside another boat well after midnight and

E

tramping over their decks to secure, does not improve tempers, particularly if they, in their turn, want to be away on the early tide while you are still in your bunk. Of course, circumstances alter cases as they say, and without specifying particular places, I am sure that you will appreciate that if you pull into one or two of the more fashionable south coast yacht harbours, although their facilities are often impeccable, it is obviously going to cost you far more per night than if you have a mooring buoy well down stream where you have half an hour's paddling to get to shore. In this, as in many other respects, the seaman's life is no different from that on shore—you get just what you are willing to pay for.

Having found your mooring buoy, I find the simplest way is to sail or motor right up to it while you are still at the tiller, grasp the buoy with your boathook *from your control position*, secure your line, and, being careful to pass the line *outside* rails and halliards, walk forward with it as you drift astern. Securing this way saves you rushing up to the sharp end hoping that the wind or tide will not push you off the buoy again, otherwise you have to rush back to your control position again and get back onto the buoy again, which is now possibly a tricky operation as you will have lost all way through the water and are virtually helpless and drifting.

This problem also occurs with the question of anchors, so we might, for this purpose, consider them under the same heading, although there are small differences in the handling.

To prevent your swinging and damage, as we have said, the ideal answer is to be secured at both ends. Remember that normally the ebbing (outgoing) tide always flows more strongly than the making (flood or incoming) tide. Principally of course because it has the natural fall of gravity to help it, like a stream dropping over a waterfall. This of course assumes no strong wind action keeping it in or encouraging it on its way out to the sea. That is why, in all this chapter on boat handling, you will be advised to approach moorings or anchorages against the tide or wind, whichever is stronger *at the time*, but you must clew up with your bows facing the ebbing (outgoing) tide, unless there is an exceptionally high wind or unusual local factors which might counteract it.

Assuming you have either lowered your anchor or secured to your buoy, allow your boat to drift astern well beyond your final position, then lower your kedge over the stern and then start hauling in on your bow cable until you are more or less equidistant between your two positions with your bows facing into the ebb-tide.

If you have two buoys, a fore-and-aft mooring as it is called, it is a good idea to have about six feet of chain cable hanging immediately below each buoy, connected by nylon line, so that having picked up one buoy, you can take the line with which you have connected the two chains, and haul yourself hand-over-hand onto the other buoy. The idea of the chain is that the line hangs down and there is no chance of the line floating or drifting and getting tied up in your or someone else's prop, keel or rudder.

ANCHORING

Before going into anchor and cable sizes, the mooring length is obviously important, and depending on wind and tide conditions, should be at least 3 to 5 times the maximum range, plus datum. Therefore, if where you intend to anchor shows 3 fathoms on your chart and the range on that day, according to your tide tables is 2 fathoms, you will need a minimum of $(3 + 2) \times 3 = 15$ fathoms (90 feet) up to $(3 + 2) \times 5 = 25$ fathoms (150 feet) if the wind gets up. So you see, you will need a large chain locker if ever you are going cruising all around our shores as there are places on the east coast with 5 fathom ranges, and approaching 7 around the Channel Islands!

You will note in the following recommended sizes of various sorts and weights of anchors and cables that chain is used. This is simply because the efficiency of an anchor just lying around on the sea-bed is of absolutely minimal value to you. Your anchor will tend to be pulled out of the sea-bed, particularly if on soft ground or mud; two to five fathoms of chain, depending on the weight of your boat, tends both to hold your anchor down and,

almost as important, prevents your rope fibre from chafing away
on sharp rocks and stones.

Finally in this chapter, the always discussable question of which
is the best type of anchor. Here are some of the main types.

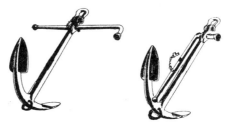

Fig. 44 Fisherman's Anchor, Ready for Use and with Stock Folded for
Stowing

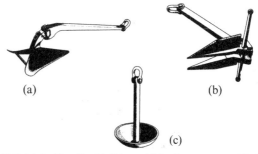

(a)   (b)

(c)

Fig. 45 'C.Q.R.' (a), 'Danforth' (b), and Mushroom-type (c) Anchors

I would generally opt for the traditional fisherman's anchor as
my main bower anchor, with a CQR kedge and either a mushroom
or Danforth but depending on where my happy hunting ground
was: on the mud or fine sand of the Thames or around Boston and
North-West Wales, or the harder sand of the Glamorganshire
coast or the rocks of the South-West and West.

Your stockless anchor really needs to be about 25 per cent
heavier than a stocked anchor, so much of the advantage of the
stowing of the one is literally outweighed by the other. A very

rough guide is that your anchor, if it is to be used under sea conditions, should be between 5 per cent and $7\frac{1}{2}$ per cent of the gross laden weight of your boat. In other words, a 5 ton cruiser should have a bower anchor of somewhere under $1\frac{1}{2}$ hundredweight and auxiliaries of about 100 pounds each.

At the base you may find a ring. If you are temporarily anchoring on a rocky bottom, it is permissible to secure your main anchor cable to this ring and let it run up the stock, but secure the top ring to the mooring rope with stout cord. Do not, of course, put the cable *through* the ring. The effect of this is that if your anchor becomes jammed in a rock crevice, you can haul taut forward, bounce up and down aft, and the leverage of the boat will snap the cord and enable you to pull the anchor up upside down. Do not *under any circumstances* do this if you are anchoring for any time, say for the night, in case the cord snaps on its own. If you wish to anchor securely for the night, attach your mooring rope to the main top ring as normal, but attach to the smaller bottom ring a fairly stout line, and buoy the top end (the old plastic one gallon can is ideal) so if you do get stuck you can move over to the buoy, pick it up and free the anchor by pulling the flukes out of the rock crevice with the lighter line, haul in your bower anchor and sail away happily with no inconvenience or embarrassment to you or anyone else (and probably feeling–and rightly so–very virtuous).

An important reminder on anchors: you *lower* your anchor over the bows once you start to drop astern, being pushed by stream or wind. You never just drop anchor, or it will drop straight to the bottom, followed by its cable which almost invariably coils itself around the anchor like a cat's cradle which will mean either that your anchor won't hold you or you'll have the job of the devil trying to get it up again. It's what is known as a foul anchor.

One more illustration of a problem of securing to a buoy. You can take it as read that there are very few places in the U.K. where, in harbour or estuary, with wind and water swinging you through 180 degrees, you will avoid either going aground, hitting a rock, or another boat. In the latter case you will *not* receive an uproarious welcome next time you use that port. In this next sketch you will see from both fish-eye and bird's-eye view what might well happen to you whilst you are fast asleep and the water level goes from high to low.

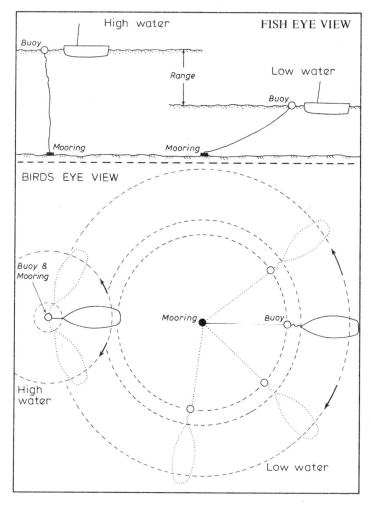

Fig. 46 Securing to a Buoy at High and Low Water

QUAYS AND JETTIES

Coming to a quay or jetty, still approach against the wind or tide stream, and securing bow first, use your engine power and lead rope as a 'spring' to force your stern against the jetty (putting out adequate fenders) and then re-berth as in this sketch.

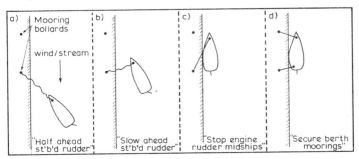

Fig. 47

If single handed, both berthing and letting go are often simpler if you secure one end of your mooring warp and pass the other end through the ring or staple, bringing it back and securing on board. Casting off is then quite easy if you pass your warp the right way in the first place.

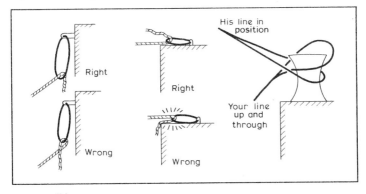

Fig. 48 Securing to Jetty Rings and Bollards

If mooring to a bollard already occupied, pass your bight up and through the other man's bight and you can all get off easily. Otherwise each one has to remove the other's before he can get free. (You may have guessed that this is the secret of many conjuring tricks with loops of string).

ANOTHER BOAT

The same method is used coming alongside another boat but put out plenty of fenders at the correct place and heights to prevent damaging her in any way.

Finally, picking up a mooring buoy single-handed can be tricky, but generally, head into wind/tide, nose up to the buoy from your control position, cut motor, grab ring with boat hook and walk forward with it as you drift astern, and secure when your bows are level. Sounds tricky, but like most things at sea, as anywhere else, quite easy if you practise, but if your judgment is wrong and you get into a bit of trouble, O.K., hard luck. You think carefully what went wrong and find that you have learned a little more about this quite unpredictable thing known as the sea; do not feel discouraged, keep trying. The only unforgiveable sin is, having made a boob, to forget and then make the same boob again. Old grey-beards might say 'seamen are born, not taught'. Whilst they might be correct to a small degree, I've seen and heard of real professionals coming adrift now and again, and the perfect skipper has not been born yet, but at least we can all try to be better than before, and think of our last attempt at mooring or anchoring.

SIX

Food and Hygiene at Sea

The galley is definitely the part of your boat that only *you* can design for the simple reason that there are those for whom half-a-dozen crates of Guinness, a dozen or so large blocks of fruit and nut chocolate and a large tin of crisps will suffice for the day, whereas there are others who intend to spend a week or more at sea and who will probably want a slightly more imaginative or exotic menu.

For the galley itself, all the average off-shore seaman needs is a large plastic bowl, deepish to avoid slopping in a seaway, and a plastic bucket with a strong, firmly attached handle to which a length of rope can be secured for the replenishing of sea water as he goes, and it needs to be strong as a two-gallon bucket in the water at seven knots is quite a strain. On the question of the eternal chore of washing up, it saves both time and temper to wipe off plates and dishes with newspaper which, at sea, can be safely ditched over the side. For the actual washing up, as fresh water is always rather a bind to get–and at some foreign ports (I think Rotterdam to be one of the worst) it is so impregnated with chlorine as to be almost undrinkable unless one is used to it; at some others a very high minimum price is placed on delivery, so if you only want ten gallons or so it can prove very dear.

Obviously, therefore, it is simpler to use sea water as much as possible, after all, there is plenty of it and it doesn't cost anything. I ask you, what is the sense in carrying two gallons of fresh water a half mile or so to your boat, much of which you are going to use to clean potatoes and cook them *and then add salt*? I consider most vegetables to taste better cooked in clean salt water anyway and just think of all the perspiration you've saved carrying the fresh water which you can now use for cleaning your teeth and making tea or coffee. I find that Teepol is as good a general additive to sea water as any, and better than most. I've always found the so-called 'sea-water' soap absolutely useless except for one thing; it's very good as a lubricant for the zip fasteners on your anoraks. Seriously!

As you will have gathered, I find that in anything much smaller than a 30–foot boat a sink is a luxurious waste of space and can be a nuisance as it is usually in the wrong place, blocks up, or is the wrong shape so that anything more than a pint or so of water in it swirls around as the boat rocks. Apart from that, if plastic it curls up if you put a hot pan in it by accident, or if of metal–or very poshly of stainless steel–either it breaks your dishes or they rattle like mad if you pile them in waiting to wash up. Far better than a sink is to have all your available space covered with a large formica-topped working surface, with your cooking pans below on shelves with vertical edges high enough to prevent them falling out, hooks or slots for your hand-tools on the bulkhead straight in front of you, and to one side, your stove. Again, whether the stove is purely a couple of rings and a grill underneath or a full oven is your choice, but in my experience the number of times that an oven is used in a boat is minimal. If you feel you must have one, have a spare source of heat and your 'oven' can be quite cheap and is really a glorified biscuit tin which not only does its job extremely well, but can be used for storage (after cleaning out of course).

Your stove must be gimballed, by which I mean on two axles, one fore-and-aft and one athwartships, so it always remains level. It should also have 'fids' or 'fiddles' which are adjustable clamps which keep your pans firmly in position on the burners. Above the cooker it is essential to have some form of fume and smell extractor, be it a simple ventilator up to the deck with a cowl which automatically turns away from the wind and therefore creates a vacuum suction, or an electrical Vent-axia type, but remember that the latter must be able to be sealed tight in a storm.

If the wind and waves are starting to get up a bit, you will probably not be cooking much anyway, but remember the poor old cook who is down there surrounded by all sorts of greasy cooking smells. He is likely to be one of the first to be affected by sea-sickness, as he does not know what is actually happening up above, just as exactly the same thing happens with car rally drivers doing the navigation. Very often men who have driven thousands of miles are car-sick by just sitting there in a rocking, rolling car and they cannot see what is going on around them, and therefore cannot brace themselves for the bumps and rolls that everyone else can see and is prepared for; so if the sea is a bit naughty (and the best cook cannot cook without hands) provide plenty of strong hand rails for him. Your plates, bowls and mugs, which are all the crockery normally needed should be stacked in racks they cannot fall out of, and should be behind and above the stove, as the best meal is ruined served on stone-cold plates.

Fire on a boat is one of the most frightening possibilities because of the moral effect it has on you—do you stay on the burning deck like the boy in the old song, or do you abandon ship and 'bail out?' Most fires start in the galley, so it is patently obvious that prevention is better than cure or loss.

A flaring deep-fat pan can be extinguished by an asbestos blanket–but one seldom has the room to stow the blanket in its special cyclinder in a small boat. The (generally) black-painted CO_2 or carbon dioxide extinguishers are good as they spray this gas onto the burning article, all oxygen is excluded and as the fire cannot occur without oxygen, the fire goes out. Sounds excellent, but if the shape of your boat and galley is such that the CO_2 simply blows straight out of the nearest exit, aided by the wind, you are back where you started from, but with an empty extinguisher; even some quite large appliances only operate under full pressure for less than twenty seconds. Dry-powder extinguishers are probably the best for a cabin, but they can make one heck of a mess; there is foam, even better, but which makes even more of a mess. *One thing that you must never do is attack an oil fire with water.* If you do that foolish thing, I assure you that you will not go down in history, you will go up in history, and with the rapidity of an Apollo rocket launcher, as boiling oil will explode with water.

When designing your galley, may I suggest that you telephone your local fire brigade, ask for the Fire Prevention Officer who, by appointment and generally without charge, but with the greatest of interest will be only too willing to advise you on the type, size, and even more important, the siting of the fire appliances for your particular boat. This advice could mean the saving of your belongings and your life.

Reverting to the fittings in the galley, there are electric fridges on the market, but they are a frightening drain on your batteries when in harbour (up to five amp load) and there are butane and propane varieties, but there are also some polystyrene types which are kept cool by the gradual evaporation of a reservoir of water on the top. These are amazingly efficient if you've got room for one, even a small one, and for keeping your milk and butter cool are first class. What is more, they cost nothing to run.

As far as cooking stoves are concerned, you have many options. Electricity is clean and convenient, but without electronic gadgetry and a couple of whacking great diesel engines to charge your batteries every few hours, this source can safely be struck off the list for the small boat man although advances are being made in this field. Advances are also being made, particularly in France and Belgium, with methylated spirit stoves which give off a lot of heat very economically. Also they have the great advantage that as meths mixes with water, if a methylated spirit stove suddenly bursts into flames through inefficient filling or a faulty valve, it can be safely extinguished by water, whereas a paraffin stove is dangerous under these circumstances as water will spread the paraffin—still burning—all over the cabin, as water and paraffin do not mix.

Many people find paraffin smelly, inconvenient and it is sometimes difficult to find a suitable grade of kerosene the other side of the Channel. So, therefore, most small boats cook, and often light, on bottled butane—or more generally these days, propane. While both these are generally excellent, they have an important snag. Both these liquid petroleum gases are heavier than air, with the result that a leaking joint or a chafed pipe allows gas to escape and to collect undetected down in the bilges, so the next cigarette you light might well be your last. Whilst this might be an efficient (and permanent) method of giving up smoking, the subsequent explosion scares the sea-birds, and it all adds to pollution. At least once a year, therefore, lift all the bilge boards and brush the whole length of pipe with washing up liquid, when all leaks will become evident.

There are patent 'sniffer' alarms on the market worked off your batteries, but it is not much use if the alarm is going on your boat moored in Poole, while you are gardening in Birmingham. You arrive on board, find a flat battery, light a cigarette while replacing the battery, and the result is much the same, both you and the boat will explode.

I understand that an inverted U–shaped tube with one end in the bilges and the other in the water facing aft acts as an automatic suction ventilator as you travel. I've never tried it, but it sounds quite reasonable.

While you have the bilge boards up, give a good clean underneath and check for smelly damp or rot. You will probably find holes drilled or moulded in the ribs to allow the water to run lengthwise aft to the bilge pump. If there are no such holes in your boat, I suggest you drill some, unless your boat is of such a shape and material as to weaken the structure by doing it. All you do is to feed a length of brass or plated chain through all the holes onto a long spring at the bow-end and you have only to raise a stern board and wiggle the chain to and fro to clear any possible obstruction so water can run straight aft and be pumped out. Water in the bilges, apart from affecting the movement of the boat as it slops as you roll, can very quickly make your bedding and shore-clothes damp and give your cabin an unwholesome smell. A small piece of someone's old nylon tights secured around the bilge-pump inlet will prevent it from blocking. I know of a case where a pump inlet blocked in heavy seas–by what would you imagine ... ? A trouser button.

As far as actual cooking is concerned, many local authorities expressly forbid it in harbour, but if allowed, remember that deep-frying in particular is for use in a flat calm only, because of the danger of spitting burning fat in a confined space, and also you will find that your blankets will seem to smell of frying for weeks afterwards.

A good, cool and generally convenient place to put your canned and bottled stores for the voyage is in the bilges, but tins and bottles with paper labels should have their contents briefly painted on. I use a number code, but always keep two lists in case one gets lost. I can assure you from personal experience which taught me this tip, there is nothing quite so off-putting as a mess of grapefruit, pilchards and pears, when you really wanted a stew of meat, potatoes and peas. Neither does a tot of vinegar taste quite the same as a tot of scotch

The sugar, coffee, flour, etc. are best put into square snap-lid boxes, clearly marked with chinagraph pencil, or better still with Dymo-tape stick-on labels.

It is surprising, but you will find that of fresh water, one gallon per day is the comfortable minimum, and up to five if you want a wash-down. Without going into the question too deeply, I have found that (and I am not trying to be unkind in any way, but just factual) a woman usually needs twice the amount of water that a man does.

Cooking at sea is always a rather thorny subject to write on for four main reasons:–

(1)   Many yachtsmen don't go (or don't intend to go) far enough to get hungry.
(2)   Some yachtsmen are so sea-sick if out in any heavy water they can't eat. (But won't mention this in public.)
(3)   They can't cook.
(4)   Their wife or some other woman is press-ganged into being galley slave for the brave sailors.

I'll deal with these four points of view in the order as given above:

NOT LONG ENOUGH AT SEA TO NEED FOOD

In theory, one can cover the seventy odd miles from, say, Weymouth to Cherbourg in about seven hours at ten knots–or ten hours at seven knots. In either case, many say, a good meal before you push off, and a packet of crisps and a bar of chocolate will do you ... or will it? Seven or ten hours in the Channel gives you one tide stream or one and a half, so navigation is pretty simple, hence few problems, but the time is bound to come when an unpredicted wind change makes you tack, and tack, and tack, and tack again and again, and fourteen or fifteen hours can well have passed without you having eaten or drunk anything of consequence.

Your engine fails, you pick up a rope or loose fishing net around your prop, part of your rigging starts to fray and needs reinforcing or replacing, or the boom reefing gear will not hold; weed or a piece of floating plastic gums itself over your cooling water inlet and makes your engine overheat. These and at least a hundred other small things mean that the tidal stream has changed direction yet again, you are well off course, the wind has changed, and you are in trouble–minor or major.

I cannot find official accurate figures, but I have read enough and spoken to sufficient qualified people to convince me that a large proportion–and I will stick my neck out and say over 65 per cent of fatalities in small boats have been preceded by one or more of the type of 'bad luck' incidents mentioned, and–on a very sombre note, I have read of several post mortem reports following deaths at sea, and most show that the bodies had virtually empty stomachs, and I am not now mentioning sea-sickness as the cause.

It is without doubt that anyone without food lacks calories, and calories represent the amount of body heat necessary for efficient working. And a hungry, cold body or mind becomes inattentive and unguarded, and it is then that one starts to make mistakes on matters so simple as to verge on the crazy or unbelievable when told while leaning on the bar at the yacht club enjoying a drink after a good meal.

Nasty it sounds, and nasty it is, but most fatalities at sea in small boats can be traced back to wrong decisions taken when the skipper's belly was as empty as a haggis packet on 2nd January.

A final but well proven warning on this subject, only a dangerous idiot or a passenger drinks at sea. A quick nip to keep out the cold so often leads to a bigger sip a quarter-hour later, a gulp after half-an-hour, and two hours later the helmsman fails to pick up say, North Lundy Light because he cannot concentrate on the twenty second gap between the double flash. If the visibility is not all that it could be, in minutes he's on a rock, and possibly we are back to to where I started this particular section–in the coroner's court on the victims.

SEA SICKNESS

I think we had better change from that rather unpleasant subject to one that is not much better, in other words sea sickness. This is the butt of the same type of twisted humour that finds it funny when a man's fly buttons or zip won't fasten, or a woman loses the support of a vital piece of elastic. It's funny for everyone else, but only someone who really has been sea sick can understand the mental as well as the physical instability of the casualty. Believe me, he is just as much a casualty as if he had received a blow on the head from the boom or twisted his ankle on the fore-deck. His only wish in life is to lean against a nice stationary lamp post for five minutes.

Don't make him into more of an idiot than he feels, and a good skipper should be on the look out for symptoms *the whole time*. Sea sickness is quite unpredictable; sometimes it takes twenty-four hours to show, sometimes lasts an hour, sometimes three days. Sometimes a man is sick, on other occasions he is not, yet under similar circumstances. There are those who say 'It's all in the mind', and I'm rather inclined to agree with them, to an extent. I have noticed that a man is never sea sick when actually under attack from an enemy and under fire. Whether he is too frightened to be sick or whether he has got something else to think about instead of himself, I do not know, and neither does anyone else, because there is no such thing as a guaranteed prevention, only palliatives which may or may not work.

However, as soon as the skipper sees the symptoms he should get the casualty to remove dentures if worn, and put them somewhere safe, because if he loses them over the side, when recovered he will feel and probably know he looks funny without them, and his trip will be ruined. Then get him to loosen tight clothing, and ensure that his life-jacket is properly secured. Sit him in the cockpit, on the lee side which is lower when he is being sick and away from the wind, but as the lee side is the lower side, snap a safety harness onto him, as if he slips over the side, he might well be too weak to do much to help himself, and keep an eye on him. Then *give him something to do*–an eyesplice to make, a burned saucepan to wire-wool out, or get him to whittle a couple of triangular bungs for the triangular holes made in fruit-juice or soup tins that are not quite finished—in fact anything to occupy his mind and to keep it off himself, and you'll both be surprised how quickly he (or she) gets over it.

Incidentally, if you are a believer in anti-sickness tablets, do not take more than the prescribed dose or they will make you frightfully thirsty and can make you dangerously drowsy. Try to ensure that your casualty keeps something in his tummy, as even if he takes sips of water and is sick again, it is still far better than being sick when there is nothing to come up; that is dreadful, and can be really painful. Once his sips of water are staying down, change to fruit-juice or soup, and when successful try Horlicks tablets or something like Marmite on toast or a biscuit. Eventually he will be able to take a few slices of toast and scrambled egg, and he's back in the crew again, feeling weak, but at least with the will to live.

Unless he's really out on his feet, in which case the skipper is gravely to blame as he should never have allowed things to get so bad without taking action, do not put him into his bunk. The smell of damp bedding, various stinks arising from the bilges plus the remnants of cooking smells will simply mean that he will lie there quietly with his eyes closed earnestly longing for death–and better

F

sooner than later. A bucket into which he has just been sick being on deck about eighteen inches under his nose does not help much either.

Seamen Who Cannot Cook

There is not a seaman who cannot cook, as cooking is just as much a part of seamanship as sewing, painting, splicing and carpentry, no matter how primitive it might be. It is one of the 'musts', and a subject I will not cover exhaustively in this book, but might expand on in a later one.

The Press-ganging of Feminine Galley Slaves

Apart from being arrogant to the point of outright rudeness, this is even worse, bad crew management. There are a few rather specialised subjects in which, arguably, one sex might be better than another, chiefly due to physical attributes of one sort or another, but to my view this does not apply generally in a small boat at sea, with the possible exception of lavatory arrangements where a certain, but not excessive, amount of lee-way must take place to avoid embarrassment by both sexes. Having said that, the (if you will please excuse the use of the word) average woman will not only equal but often better her male counterpart in navigation and chart-work and her accuracy and finesse is frequently certainly equal to a man's in keeping a wayward boat on to a strict bearing over long distances where pin-point attentiveness to the wavering compass-card is so important for the hoped for land fall.

A woman frequently has to cook for fifty weeks out of the year, and not only is it daft to confine her to the galley for the other two, but given half a chance she will make as good a seaman as anyone else on board and enjoy herself, and can still spare a few seconds to shout instructions down to the cook while he does the cooking.

I am not saying this as a women's liberation crusader–I refuse to burn any of my underclothing on principle–but if she is good enough to be a crew member, she must be trained as a crew member, because if an accident happens to the male crew, how can she get you home if you have never taken the trouble to show her how?

I know it might be a blow to your prestige to have to admit in public that you had twisted your ankle and that the impeccable way in which your boat was brought up all-standing to the buoy, made fast, sails stowed and boom secured was all done by your wife, but you can always claim the prestige of having taught her–if you're that sort of man!

SEVEN

'Here is the Weather Forecast . . . '

Scientists now know almost all that there is to know about weather, and even confer learned degrees upon those who have studied it for years. The only thing, however, that they do not know for absolutely certain, is what causes its alterations and when they are going to occur in any one place–which really means that they do not know very much about it.

Mark Twain is reputed to have said; 'Everyone always talks about the weather, but nobody ever does anything about it.' But to be fair, millions of pounds are spent internationally, and scientists are using very expensive and sophisticated instruments searching for reasons why.

Although not knowing the cause of weather changes, no one complained about the many glorious sunny days of midsummer 1975, although we did get snow in June that year, and torrential rainstorms and floods later.

However, when the traditional damp of winter drags its sunless sodden course into spring and summer, and continues to ooze its wet and windswept way into autumn and yet another miserable winter, we are apt to attribute cause to either one or more of the following:–

(1) The Government (of any political colour).
(2) The Common Market (it used to be Adolph Hitler, then General de Gaulle).
(3) Nuclear bomb explosions (used to be Atom bombs).
(4) Sun spots or explosions either on the surface of the sun or in the fiery atmosphere surrounding it, which affect its heat emission to us.

(5) The roof of carbon dioxide surrounding the earth which is being increased to terrifying proportions by the burning of fossil fuels such as coal and oil.

(6) Pollution of all sorts from tetraethyl lead and tetramethyl lead from motor spirit to water vapour from refrigerators and detergents from washing machines.

There are also various types of dusts, plus nitrous oxide, sulphur dioxide and many other gases, all of which have some effect on one or more of the range of light rays from infra-red to ultra-violet that we receive from the sun.

All that we know with absolute certainty is that changes in the normal pattern of weather in any one part of the world are basically controlled by the amount of light and heat received from the sun, and where it is received on earth.

As the sun is so far away, we can fairly assume its rays to be parallel for all practical purposes. To give you a brief glimpse at the comparisons, Mercury is the nearest planet to the sun, a mere thirty-six million miles, and Pluto the most distant, a slightly more formidable mileage of over 3,600 million. O.K., you say, so what the heck? What about the fact that in our solar system, which includes both those two, (puny earth coming outside Mercury and Venus but inside Mars) the sun consists of nearly 99.9 per cent of the mass in the system. Staggering isn't it? Anyway, I trust that the next time the weather forecasters are wrong in your little patch of the solar system when you had an outside 'do' of some sort on, you will remember that weather is difficult to predict on a large range, and verging on the impossible (or dodgy) on a local scale for any longish period ahead.

I had a cousin who was an underwriting member of Lloyds of London, and the financial success or failure of an open-air reception abroad depended on the attendance of royalty. My cousin bet on the British Met. Office and made money, whereas the local forecasters (in Australia, in fact, before the 1939 to 1945 war) were very wrong over the long time range. However, it is quite easily possible to foretell local weather for about five to six hours or so ahead, which is all you really need to either run for shelter or prepare for a blow.

Reverting to the sun's effect, you will see from the next sketch that the rays of light have less distance to penetrate at the equator than at the poles, where the distance through the atmosphere is considerablly more than the twenty odd miles high that the ever-decreasing density of the atmosphere reaches vertically, hence a part reason for the difference in temperature between the equator and the poles.

Mathematicians amongst you might be interested to know the completely useless piece of information that this covering contains some $1\frac{1}{2}$ million tons of air for each of the earth's inhabitants. You wouldn't think so when your neighbour's garden fire is smoking you out of house and home would you?

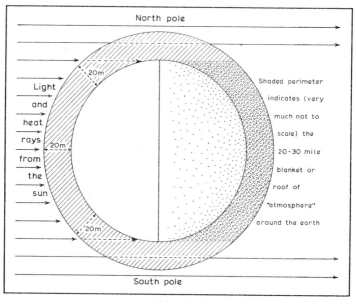

Fig. 49

Anyway, the sun shines on the air around and above us, and warms the air more quickly than the land, the land more quickly than the large inland water systems, or the sea, and when the air is heated it expands, which gives us three main effects.

Firstly, the air becomes lighter as the same amount of air is taking more space; secondly, while expanded and lighter it therefore rises above denser cooler air; and thirdly, as it expands, it compresses adjoining air, thus giving it a higher pressure, which makes it want to move into an area of lower pressure, in rather the same way as you can flip a melon seed by pressing it between your thumb and forefinger.

It is this pressure that makes the air want to escape into a less constricted area, and when it does just this, we call the result wind.

Weather-ships provided by many maritime nations sit in more or less fixed positions, literally come hell or high water in order to warn, or to confirm other reports, of what is going on with the world's winds, and they do this twenty four hours a day, 365 (or 366) days a year. These ships regularly send up balloons, sometimes more than twelve feet in diameter, which contain a very carefully measured amount of helium gas. The weight of helium is known of course, and just the correct amount is fed into the balloons to keep them aloft and steady in altitude to within about a hundred feet or so, and follow any particular high altitude wind currents which the scientists want to study. They generally have the odd chunk of electronic gadgetry dangling from them, which, after the signals are interpreted by the boffins, produce all sorts of information on what the balloon is 'seeing' up there. At least one of these balloons has been constantly transmitting information for over a year.

Some belts of rapidly moving air are very high in the sky and known as jet-streams. Cases are recorded where jet aircraft at 30 to 40,000 feet can cut the time of east-bound New York to London journey by over an hour. Ships, particularly the old square-riggers, have been using known seasonal winds and currents for hundreds of years, as of course, migrating birds have done since they could fly, but we have much yet to learn about the limitless area surrounding our puny universe, and our slowly increasing ability to travel in it.

But to revert to our problems on this tiny spinning ball which we call earth, let's think further of the high pressure to low pressure air movement, wind.

You will *never* get weather trouble out of a clear blue sky, as it is only when clouds are formed from the heat differences that things start to happen. As the sun's rays heat and suck up 1,000 million tons of water per day (give or take a gallon or so) this is all turned to water vapour and deflected towards the East by the rotation of the earth, rises, cools, and sinks back to the earth at about 30° degrees North and South latitudes, as you can see in the next sketch. These main winds remain pretty constant. See Fig. 50.

The British Isles lie mostly between 50° degrees North and 60° degrees North and you will see that our winds are predominantly from the South-West and quite often from the North-East. but only on exceptional occasions do they blow for long periods from the North-West or South-east.

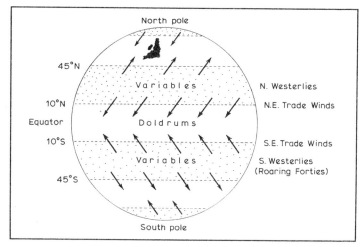

Fig. 50 Barometric Pressure or Climatic Zones showing Shaded Belts of High Pressure moving into Low Pressure Areas

When the temperature of surface water gets warm enough it changes into water vapour, which for sea use is offically designated mist at surface level when the visibility is limited to one nautical mile, and fog when visibility decreases to a half-mile (1,000 yards). This water vapour rises and falls, changes shape and colour and direction and blows in different directions at different heights, even turning to ice crystals high up. *This is why instant recognition of the type of cloud is vital to a seaman,* because it is this combination of height, size, shape, colour, direction and speed of movement that gives him the essential clues to the type of weather of which he might well be on the receiving end of for the next few hours. I stress only a few hours, as your observations are only local, but using a barometer and thermometers, and keeping a good weather eye open, you might well be correct for up to twelve hours or more.

When you walk into your car or into your garden or, in short, any time you are out in what used to be known as 'God's own fresh air' (although it is only found in limited amounts these days on land) get into the habit of looking upwards, compare what you see with these following drawings and you will surprise yourself at how much knowledge you will pick up in a very short time.

so watch it, and stand by
to secure gear, batten down
and stand by for a blow.

The Cirrus range is pretty high, generally above 18,000 feet, the Alto range usually from 8,000 feet to 18,000 feet, and the Strato below. The Cumulus range can either be low and flatish or bubbly, or can tower to great heights in storms. For use at the same time as looking at these cartoon-type drawings of cloud types, here is a list of old fish-wives' tales about the weather, many of which are very reliable, and some of which are not always so true, but you will be beginning to judge their reliability by their cause yourself soon.

Light scudding clouds on their own—wind—(altocumulus)
Light clouds, low under and heavier above—wind and rain—(cumulonimbus). (Cont. on page 95.)

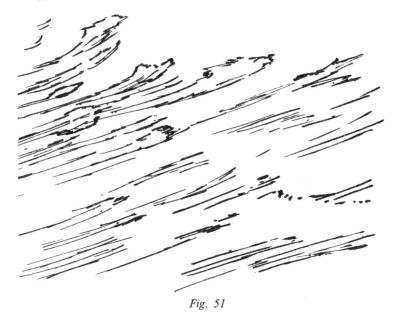

Fig. 51

(1) CIRRUS–Light, feathery, silky, and very high, often composed of detached masses of tiny ice crystals. When little tufts lie to leeward end on top are sometimes called 'Mares' Tails'. Weather settled at the moment, but watch for signs of dropping to a lower level.

Fig. 52
(2) CIRROCUMULUS–In transparent flaky layers, usually without shadows, resembling a mackeral (before it is tomatoed and canned) or the ripples left in the sand at low water.

Fig. 53
(3) CIRROSTRATUS–Thin, web-like veil giving a milky looking effect. Often completely covers the sky, and sun or moon show but are generally surrounded by a halo. (See ALTO-STRATUS). Only practice will tell you the difference).

Fig. 52

Fig. 53

Fig. 54

Fig. 54
(4) ALTOCUMULUS–In thin layers or patches, often just touching. Rather vague and difficult to place exactly. Usually lightly shaded.

Fig. 55
(5) ALTOSTRATUS–Thicker than CIRROSTRATUS above and blue-grey in colour. Possibility of drizzle or steady light rain. Vague position of sun can generally be seen.

Fig. 56
(6) STRATOCUMULUS–Bulky layers or patches tending to twist or roll–grey with darker shadings and in fairly soft regular globular masses. A bad sign if coming towards you. Watch for change to CUMULONIMBUS.

Fig. 55

Fig. 56

Fig. 57

Fig. 57

(7) STRATUS–Like low fog. When breaking up is called FRACTO-STRATUS–a good sign.

Fig. 58

(8) NIMBOSTRATUS–Low uniformly dark grey. Usually raining steadily. Typically British winter day, often preceded by CIRROSTRATUS and ALTOSTRATUS. Often accompanied by low ragged patches.

Fig. 59

(9) CUMULUS–Large and rising rather like a good fluffy omelette, with its rounded top with flat base. If sun shining, light and shade alternate vividly. Weather changeable so watch carefully for change of colour to darker CUMULONIMBUS. If top breaks off and sweeps up to CIRRUS you can feel happier and hope for a good day's sailing.

Fig. 58

Fig. 59

Black clouds–rain–(nimbostratus).

High, soft, delicate,(fluffy masses–fine–(culmulus).

Hard, inky coloured clouds with sharp outlines–rain, probably wind–(cumulonimbus).

Misty (clouds over hills, staying or lowering–wind, if rising, improving–(stratus).

Higher clouds blown in different direction from lower ones–wind will strengthen towards the direction of the upper clouds.

Yellow sunset–rain

Rosy sunset–fine

Bright, clear dawn–generally settled

Dawn breaking over low clouds on horizon–rain

Fog and/or dew–rain or wind very unlikely

Clear visibility and audibility–rain

Red dawn–wind

Purple dawn–wind and rain–possible storm

Fig. 60

(10)   CUMULONIMBUS–Heavy and dark and definitely anvil-shaped at the top with the flat-topped CIRRUS stemming out of blackish CULMUS.
Thundery and could be naughty.

You must have seen the weather man on the 'telly' scores of times, with his map of the British Isles with lines and mystic signs all over it, which he points to almost proudly (no personalities meant) as he talks about warm and cold fronts, depressions, cyclones, and other odd-sounding things. I happen to know that they realize that their prognostications are not getting home to about 95 per cent of their viewers, but, alas, they are limited in time and cannot fully explain in the amount available what is being explained to you in this chapter. So please do not blame the poor bloke, he is doing the best he can and teaching (literally) to the converted, in other words, to the few who take the trouble to learn the pretty simple facts of how weather works. I know there are books galore written about the subject in detail, but at the end of this chapter at least I can promise you that you will be 'with' the weatherman all the way.

As a matter of fact, it is rather fun (and you can always take side-bets on your success with your kids or friends) to see if you can be one step ahead of him, or better still for your ego, to prove him wrong–in your area at least.

All you do is have a blank map of the British Isles with the weather reporting stations marked on it. In fact it is simpler and better to get yourself some 'metmaps' (Form No. 2216) only one penny each, from H.M. Stationary Office. You then listen to the BBC's 'Reports from Coastal Stations', the times and wave-length being in the *Radio Times*. (See also chapter on radio). These reports are given in clockwise rotation and you simply fill in the figures of the barometric pressure at each station as given, plus where you are at the time, from your own transmitter, and note the wind directions.

After a little practice you will be able to draw in the lines joining the stations where they report the same pressure–the curves you draw being called ISOBARS. (Iso comes from the Greek meaning 'same' and, as you will find later, it is used in several other branches of sea science.) Sometimes pressures are given in 2 millibar or 4 millibar intervals depending on the size of the area you are studying, so obviously the odd numbers should be half-distanced between the evenly numbered ones.

G

From my sketch you will see how the line joining the stations with 994 millibars swerves down in the Atlantic, forming a low area known as a depression, of 989 millibars. After all, don't you feel low when you're depressed? After a little practice at this game, you will be able to guess the remaining lines to fit in with the general weather flow as you see it. Each time you listen to the coastal reports, therefore, you can see how your low areas (generally bad) and your high areas (generally good) are progressing.

This sketch shows rather an unhealthy position, because as the prevailing wind is usually from the south-west in this country as we have already seen, and on this occasion the high area of 1000 millibars is over France, I would not make a trip of more than an hour or two unless I were prepared, equipped and crewed ready to take on what might prove to be rather a lot of salt water all over the place.

Reverting to our metmap, the distance *between* the isobars is important too, as, rather like contour lines on a map, the nearer together they are the steeper or harder the winds flowing between them are likely to be.

This can be measured by what is called a 'geostrophic scale', which is printed on the sides of metmaps, so your drawings will build up showing your probable general weather picture, or at least where danger is likely to come from and how severe it might be, and it is the series, not just a 'one-off' that is valuable to you.

The basis of weather forecasting depends on currents of air of differing pressures/temperatures meeting, this line of meeting being called a 'front'.

Let us take this situation to bits in two typical circumstances, and you will see, I hope, how it works from sea-level.

Let us have the good news first then. When you are in choppy water with coolish air and slight rain and as always noting the barometer which has been rising at about one millibar for the last two-three hours, you might find that the rain turns to drizzle, then to fog and mist, and suddenly you burst out into clear sunlight with calm seas. This is what has been happening to you. See Fig. 52.

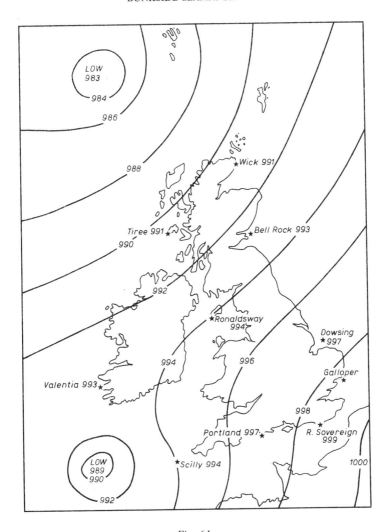

Fig. 61

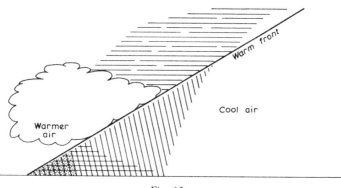

Fig. 62

Now for the bad news which shows why weather usually turns bad more quickly than it turns good, and you will see the curve in this next sketch. The reason for this is, as we all know that warm air tends to rise, the cold air tends to advance upon you like a wall, not a sloping improvement as in the last sketch.

Fig. 63

These two sketches sum up the rhyme:–

> When the wind's before the rain
> Soon you may make sail again.
> But when the rain's before the wind
> Halyards, sheets and braces mind.

Air pressure is usually measured in one of two ways, with the mercury barometer or the aneroid barometer. In the following sketches you will see both the crudest idea of how they work and what the tools themselves actually look like.

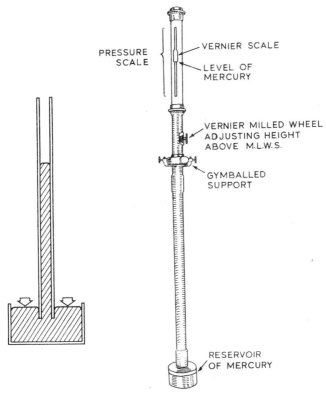

PRESSURE SCALE

VERNIER SCALE

LEVEL OF MERCURY

VERNIER MILLED WHEEL ADJUSTING HEIGHT ABOVE M.L.W.S.

GYMBALLED SUPPORT

RESERVOIR OF MERCURY

Fig. 64 Mercury Barometer

The mercury barometer is the more accurate of the two, and is the one usually used in weather stations ashore and afloat, and in larger ships both fighting and merchant, but the long glass tube is obviously more susceptible to damage by shock so has to be treated with great care. A reasonably priced aneroid barometer is quite sufficient for a small boat's needs though, particularly if it is set accurately in the first place.

This is simply enough done by comparing the reading with the barometer usually found outside the harbour master's offices, coastguard and lifeboat stations. You subtract 0.01 inches or 0.37 millibars for every 10 feet their barometer is placed above mean sea level. You then add the same again to get the pressure right for the height at which it will be placed in your boat and there you are with your barometer correctly set.

The necessity for adjustment of a newly fitted barometer will become obvious when one considers that until comparatively recently an aircraft's altimeter was simply a barometer which showed height above sea level by diminishing air pressure as the aircraft went up and up. The airman then did crafty bits of map reading to see what hill they were flying over, subtracted its height and the result was the distance to 'ground floor level'.

Sometimes you will find barometers measured in inches of mercury, or in millibars, so here is a brief conversion table from which you will see that 5 millibars is approximately 0.15 inches of mercury. Millibars are almost universally used these days and I would recommend you to stick an amended scale on an 'inch measurement' barometer.

As the water vapour expands and forms into clouds, it also has the power to hold even more water vapour. The humidity in the air alters tremendously from, say Kuwait in the Persian Gulf where it is very hot but very dry, to the South-East Asian jungle where the air holds so much water that it can become saturated and when it is holding as much as it can, any cooling forms instant condensation back to mist or fog or rain. Enthusiasts can get a lot of interest and information from a 'wet and dry bulb thermometer', technically called a hygrometer. This is simply two

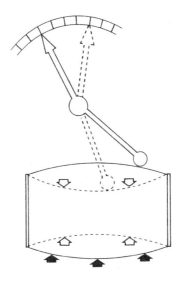

Fig. 65 Aneroid Barometer

INCHES	MILLIBARS
28.05	950
28.20	955
28.35	960
28.50	965
28.64	970
28.79	975
28.94	980
29.09	985
29.23	990
29.38	995
29.53	1000
29.68	1005
29.83	1010
29.97	1015
30.12	1020
30.27	1025
30.42	1030
30.56	1035
30.71	1040
30.86	1045
31.01	1050

identical thermometers side by side, one placed normally, the other with the bottom end stuck into a wad of cotton wool or similar which is kept soaked by a little reservoir kept full of plain water. Normally of course, water is cooler than its surrounding air, and evaporation causes more cooling (which is the theory of your refrigerator) so the thermometers will show different readings, but the figures will get closer together as the humidity level rises, and when identical you have your 100 percent humidity, or saturated air.

If you have a hygrometer in your boat it will give you an excellent guide to the possibility of fog, and the wind direction at the time will tell you from which direction it is likely to clear.

Another useful tool if you can afford it (or if you've got room for it) is an anemometer or wind gauge. Obviously you have to treat its readings with reserve and adjust them to take into account the wind you are making yourselves by travelling along, or 'the wind you feel' and 'the wind you make'. Subtract the two and you have the true wind speed. A simpler way is to stop! Seriously though, when you are starting on this game of guessing wind speed at sea, there is not much sense in sucking your forefinger and pointing it aloft and expecting a divination from spirits above (or below according to your religion) to tell you, for example, 'Wind Beaufort Scale 5, speed 19 knots, direction 202 degrees'.

A little catch here, though, please do not forget that Southwesterly wind comes from the South-west, whereas a Southwesterly tide stream goes to the South-west. Sorry about that, but I didn't make the rules and that's the way it's been for many years and I'm sure that even after decimalisation and metrication, they won't change that one. There is probably a simple logic to it somewhere, but I've never come across it in my time at sea, although someone else probably has and will tell me.

Once at sea, you should take a careful reading of your barometer and note it in your Log at least once every two hours, or every hour if changing rapidly. Under ideal conditions your readings should be steady on at least 1013 millibars, but a steady drop of three millibars over three hours could well mean the possibility of South to South-west wind veering to West to Northwest and worsening, possibly to gale force. If you remember the rule 'left right–high low' it means that, *in the Northern Hemisphere,* if you face the wind, the area of High Pressure is to your left, and to your right is the Low pressure area into which the wind is funnelling, but due to the rotation of the earth it is swung slightly eastwards; facing the wind therefore, the centre of any storm disturbance is to your right, so obviously you try to avoid having the wind coming over your port side or you will probably be heading straight into the centre of the storm.

Herewith the famous Admiral Beaufort's scale of wind forces and descriptions which he laid down in 1805 (Sir Francis was barely twenty-five years old) and is still in almost international use today, nearly one and threequarter centuries later.

NOTE:　　The wave heights shown on this scale are the average found in the open sea, but in in-shore waters, the effects of wind and tide may make the wave heights less but much steeper, thus more dangerous. All these figures, therefore, must be used as a comparative guide only and not as certainty.)

The Beaufort Scale has three main uses; it tells how big the seas *really* are, for even a six foot wave looks big from a small boat; it makes a comparative 'norm' for BBC weather forecasters; and last but not least, it is a convenient method of noting weather conditions in your ship's log.

Finally, looking at your barometer *once* means next to nothing as it is the progression of pressures up or down and the height and type of cloud, and the direction of the wind which will give you the essential clues to enable you to keep out of trouble. If a sudden storm does burst upon you unawares, you have two options open to you; make for shelter (*if you are absolutely sure you can make it in time.*) If there be any doubt, you are far better advised to get away from a lee-shore to get plenty of sea room to play with, take in reefs if under sail, batten down hatches, close scuttles (or portholes), lash down all loose gear, have a sea-anchor and/or drogue ready to stream, take a double check on your exact position and on the direction and speed of tidal streams, check the easy availability of any distress flares and dinghy if carried, and stand by to ride it out (wearing your life-jacket of course). This is 'boat handling'.

It is unfortunate that many small-boat owners consider anything above a moderate breeze as dangerous, but if you have trust and confidence in your boat and your handling of it, and you have worked up the experience yourself it is surprising the wind and waters that you can take in your stride. It is nothing like as dangerous as driving a car, but the casualty figures (see S.A.R.) are only figures and do not show that most road accidents are caused

BEAUFORT WIND SCALE

Wind Scale No.	Wind Speed (Knots)	Title	Description of Sea Surface	Probable Mean Wave Height Metres	Feet	Probable Max. Wave Height Metres	Feet
0	Less than 1	Calm	Mirror like	—	—	—	—
1	1–3	Light air	Ripples but no foam crests	0.1	0.3	0.1	0.5
2	4–6	Light breeze	Small wavelets, crests with glassy look but not breaking	0.2	0.5	0.3	1
3	7–10	Gentle breeze	Large wavelets, crests starting to break into glassy foam, possibly occasional 'white horse'	0.6	2	1.0	3
4	11–16	Moderate breeze	Small waves and longer with fairly frequent 'white horses'	1.0	3	1.5	5
5	17–21	Fresh breeze	Moderate waves, noticeably longer with 'white horses' occasionally flicking off into spray	2.0	6	2.5	9
6	22–27	Strong breeze	Larger waves and more extensive foaming crests with more frequent spray. Uncomfortable in small boat	3.0	9	4.0	13
7	28–33	Near gale	Sea gives appearance of piling up, crests start to be blown into streaks by wind	4.0	14	5.5	19
8	34–40	Gale	Waves moderately high and longer. Crests blown into spindrift streaking with the wind	5.5	18	7.5	25
9	41–47	Strong gale	High waves with crests beginning to topple over, spray increasing and possibly affecting visibility	7.0	23	10.0	32
10	48–55	Storm	Very high waves with crests overhanging and tumbling. Surface takes a white appearance and jarring becomes noticable when wave hits boat	9.0	29	12.5	41
11	56–63	Violent storm	Small medium sized ships possibly lost to view behind very high waves, sea completely covered by long patches of foam, foam affecting visibility badly	11.5	37	16.0	52
12	64–71	Hurricane	Air filled with foam and spray, sea completely white and bubbling in appearance. Driving spray very seriously affecting visibility	14.0	45		
13	72– 80						
14	81– 89		The hurricane				
15	90– 99		conditions become				
16	100–108		progressively worse				
17	109–117						

Fig. 66 Beaufort Wind Scale

by carelessness, whereas most sea accidents are caused by ignorance of one factor or another.

Often if a boat is in trouble, it started with the skipper, so the choice is ultimately with YOU, if you are the skipper, so phone the coastguard by all means and get his opinion (no charge), but *you* are the skipper who carries the can and only you know what experience you have had, so if in doubt, don't go out.

EIGHT

The Seaway Code

Rather unfortunately for the injured or damaged sailor or swimmer, there is no *compulsory* third party insurance, such as with road vehicles, nor for that matter is there any comparable legislation of that type covering private boats, although it might well be forced upon us by necessity if 'the water-hog' continues to be permitted to charge around regardless of the safety, comfort and well-being of others. In fact, this has already been mentioned by at least one Member of Parliament, and with altruistic and not political interests in mind, is receiving a lot of support from the professional seamen and members of the various search and rescue (S.A.R.) organizations.

I can only presume that laws have not been brought in because of the difficulty of affixing car-type registration plates to the many types, shapes and sizes of vessels, and the potential cost of maritime policemen in 'panda-boats', who, I expect would probably be nicknamed 'aqua-fuzz'.

Sailing boats belonging to a standard type have their class mark (an interesting study on their own); their individual registered number is on the sail, so the name of the owner of a class boat is registered by the club or association of that class. There is nothing the slightest bit snobbish about this, as one can buy a class boat in kit form for around a hundred pounds or less, but you cannot buy a 'class' car in those terms of money.

Professional fishing boats are also registered, but at their ports of origin, and have two letters, usually the first and last letters of the port painted in large white letters and figures on their bows;

thus, Poole could well have a boat numbered PE 123, and Brixham a BM 234. These letters are not invariably the first and last of their port, as obviously some duplication arises in spelling of ports, as in *P*ortsmout*h* and *P*lymout*h*, or *G*alwa*y* and *G*rimsb*y*, but a sensible compromise is made where the port of origin is usually unmistakeable.

Although it is not strictly necessary to license or 'register' a private craft of less than forty tons, I would advise you to register it, and full details of how to go about it, and how much it will cost are readily available from your local Customs and Excise Office. Registration has the great advantages that (a) When you get a ship-to-shore radio, you have a call-sign, which is usually your registered number, (b) Your numbers are registered in *Lloyd's Register of Shipping* and therefore your signal flags give your name and port of origin, and (c) Your entry to foreign countries is greatly eased by having Ship's Papers. Further details on this are given in the H.M. Customs and Excise section of S.A.R. later on in the book.

There are also, however, laid down '*Rules for Preventing Collisions at Sea*', and these require really careful study, particularly this chapter on giving-way action and movements dealing with the 'priority' of sailing or power boats which might be in your course. In a moment, I will explain why I have written 'priority' within quotation marks. The following few rules are only a primer to the complete rules.

The primary obligation for power-boats is that *you keep to your right* of oncoming vessels at sea, and always keep right in harbours, rivers and canals, unless specifically ordered not to do so; hence, you pass an approaching vessel port to port, and as the wheel, particularly of a power-craft is usually on the port side, you can exchange pleasantries (or otherwise if your whim so decides) with the approaching skipper. You won't get mixed on which side to go if you keep in mind the fact that the other chap is making for his port, and that you (DV) want to get back to yours in one piece, so the old rule port to port makes good sense.

Most boats under power have screws turning clockwise when

viewed from astern, and because of this rotation, the boat tends to turn more rapidly to starboard than to port, so remember, boat in sight–turn right (unless turning into more danger).

Having said that there is little legislation, this statement refers only to pleasure craft which carry no passengers or cargo 'for hire or reward', in which case there are stringent rules laid down by the Department of Trade and H.M. Customs. These bodies have the power to stop and search any vessels about whose 'legal rights in British territiorial waters' they might have reason to doubt.

While I wish in no way to get embroiled with the question of territorial limits, be they concerning fishing rights or oil rigs, it would be wise of you to remember that the statement 'I was over three miles out of Exmouth, just about level with Torquay, in fact', might seem to you to be a reasonable statement as not being much more than three miles off-shore. However, the territorial waters of most countries *exclude* bays and estuaries, but are taken from prominent points such as Portland Bill and Start Point, so you might be well out of the three-mile limit from shore, but it is well over twenty miles before you cross the line joining Start Point to Portland Bill.

To really rub the danger of this subject in to you, be very careful that you know exactly where you stand if you happen to have on board a guest who does not possess a full British passport. It could be quite innocent, but it does make you look a bit of a fool if things are not quite as they seem, and you get a write-up in the Sunday newspapers.

In fact, H.M. Customs and Excise are not that daft, and if, in fact, you had been on that particular game, they would have had their eyes upon you for a considerable time, but mistakes can happen, and please check any guests you may have on board if you are going off-shore. As in most laws, governmental, catholic, civic or any of the others, ignorance of a law is not accepted as an excuse for breaking it. It might seem hard, but that's the way the cookie crumbles, as they say.

To change the aspect, but to keep to the same subject, at this moment, (1977), if one of H.M. Coastguard sees a flagrant disregard of the rules of seamanlike conduct before his very eyes, there is very little–apart from warning signals–that he can do about it. He might possibly be called as an expert witness in a common-law action in open court taken by the aggrieved party for personal damages or repairs to his boat and subsequent expenses, but H.M. Coastguard *is in no way* a maritime policeman. His responsibility is search and rescue, and extends very little further, (unfortunately).

This might seem to be an unsatisfactory state of affairs, (and this is purely my personal point of view), but, as treading on one man's liberty must affect the equal liberty of the other man to tread on that same liberty, the question becomes either academic, or political, and as I am neither academically or politically motivated, I'll bow out, and let you think it over when you've got the time, and if you consider it important anyway.

It is interesting to note, still keeping to the legal angle, that in the official *International Regulations for Preventing Collisions at Sea*, none of the laws give any non-official vessel any 'rights'; the regulations merely specify that, in cases of doubt, which boat, under certain circumstances, 'shall keep clear of the other'. It does not in any way indicate, or intimate, that the one boat has priority over the other.

This is a very subtle difference, I agree, but as the law at sea, as on land *is* subtle in its meaning, always remember that, basically, you *never* have the right or priority in the generally accepted meaning of the word, but that as you will see later in this chapter, you must give way under certain cases.

These Regulations referred to were drawn up by several of the leading maritime nations of the world early in this century, and have been amended as necessary on several occasions since, as other nations have become more interested, and safety-conscious, and have also started to participate, principally in 1910, 1931, 1969, and a conference of the Sea in 1976.

In 1969 the Greek and Russian delegates agreed to altered meanings to be given to individual flag signals, together with the international phonetic alphabet now used in eleven languages as further explained in the chapter on flags and signals, and it now appears that the international code is becoming more truly international with fewer nations opting out.

All seamen of all nations will be both happier and safer in their dangerous work when all maritime nations undertake their full responsibilities.

The international regulations, (which are themselves reinforced by the British Merchant Shipping Acts) consist of no less than thirty-eight rules divided into four distinct parts:–

(A) Preliminary and definitions
(B) Lights and shapes
(C) Steering and sailing rules
(D) Miscellaneous

However, don't get worried, I'm not going to set them down word for word, or even include all the regulations, for the simple reason that they are so formulated (as is right and proper, I suppose) as to apply to all conceivable types of shipping in every part of the world, and this includes cases where a sea-plane must carry lights not normally carried by a swan or a wild goose, but who tells who and which gives to which?

Basically, these rules must be so formulated as to apply to all types of vessels (N.B. no differential between boats and ships, they are almost invariably referred to as vessels), but they are mentioned by their length, or their occupation. Many of the thirty-two rules referred to would not apply to your craft, but included in another chapter is , for example, the lights which must be shown by tugs towing several barges astern or alongside. Although you probably do not expect to be towing many barges with *your* boat, the lights should at least ring a bell with you, and I'll tell you exactly why.

If you can imagine travelling quietly up the Lower Thames on a still night, enjoying your trip, and watching your buoys flashing ahead, and planning your course, you could well be forgiven for thinking that you were having hallucinations when you suddenly got the impression that somehow the whole of Liverpool Docks

H

had broken loose from its moorings, and by some obscure route was now floating *en masse* down the Thames towards you, with the lights of Tower Bridge before you, and the Houses of Parliament showing clearly over the top.

Anything tending towards the impossible verges on the frightening until the simple truth dawns, and in this case, it was simply a string of barges being towed both astern and alongside the tug.

Reverting to the more serious, I trust you will forgive me for rubbing in the important regulations that other seamen you meet up with will expect you to know, otherwise they might well mutter to themselves.'That —— has got no right to be at sea, he (or she) is a —— menace'. And, remember, he could be right.

In this chapter I'll give some of the *preliminary definitions of some* of the steering and sailing rules, but you will find that those not specifically mentioned here are elsewhere, in one of the chapters more concerned with that particular problem.

First of all, there are very different sets of Rules strictly applicable to (1) sailing boats, and (2) powerboats; this means that if you suddenly see Admiral Lord Nelson's H.M.S. *Victory* coming towards you with a 50 cubic capacity outboard motor over her stern, even if *Victory* has all her many sails fully set, that outboard motor puts her into the powered boat classification in the eyes of the maritime legal eagles. So always watch the wake of a sailing vessel, and you will soon learn to distinguish if she is re-inforcing her sail-power with an engine, in which case you treat her in all respects as if she were a power-boat. When it comes to the question of who gives way to whom, although basis common-sense if not specifically mentioned in the regulations, one is expected to use it.

This rule is, of course, put in to protect those who by virtue of being entirely wind-powered cannot help themselves, in that a pure sailing vessel (regardless of size) can only sail within certain limits.

On the other hand, if a motor is running, of any size from the *QE2*'s turbines down to a tiny outboard, she is, to a larger or smaller extent, an agent free of the dictates of the wind, and is therefore a powerboat.

As with many other things at sea, the rules of warning by horn or klaxon come in groups of three, one blast for right, two blasts for left, and three blasts for 'engines going astern'. If therefore, a vessel is in your course and obviously having difficulty in turning in a confined area, if you lose your temper and bear down on her at a rate of knots giving three loud blasts on your hooter as if to say 'Get out of my —— way', she will (quite correctly) ignore you as she will have accepted your signal that you have appreciated her difficulties, and are going astern, and later she will no doubt graciously thank you for your courtesy. Point taken?

As with motor driving, it is very frequently the lack of forethought and lack of courtesy more than lack of knowledge. In a recent survey of motorists, over 80 percent considered themselves above average. Delightful mathematics, isn't it? Yet again reverting to motoring similes, the driver of a Jaguar must make allowances for the wind and road effect of a moped, which has just as much right to the road as he has, and for the very different difficulties of the heavy goods driver.

In other words, no matter how adept you might be in the handling of *your* craft, you will never be a seaman until you can at least understand, and learn to make allowances for, the differences in the handling techniques of other types of craft.

Another very important distinction to be made clear is that a vessel (for the purposes of the regulations) is under way when she is not connected to the seabed or to any other fixed object such as a quay or another securely moored vessel. I do not include 'not under command', as that generally infers that a ship is aground, or is in other difficulties, and flies signal flags, cones or lights to denote this.

Thus, you see, your boat can be under way, but stationary in the water. Do not confuse this phrase with *under weigh* as this latter phrase simply means that the anchor is broken out of the ground, some of the anchor weight is on her anchor cable, and the vessel is just about ready to take in her cable, and be away to sea. Another phrase used in the same context is 'cable up-and-down', that is, vertical, and not lying on the seabed.

That is all on the preliminaries, you'll probably be glad to know, so now for the rules that affect you. Now and again I will include the number of the regulation for those who want to learn all of the thirty-two for the D.O.E. certificate mentioned in the introduction.

In all the following sketches, it is asssumed that the wind comes from the left in each case, and the sailing craft is shown with her sail boom out roughly in the appropriate direction, and the powered craft shows her propeller wake, and each case the rough angle of the rudder. Also, in each sketch the *black* boat is the one which should give way to the *white* one, to avoid collision.

Fore-and-aft type, in other words modern sailing boats are at their most vunerable with the wind astern. You will see if you study the following sketches that movement of the rudder or tiller bar away from the wind involves a smooth movement of the sail boom across the boat, the effect of the wind lessening as the boat comes up to face into it, but increasing again as she starts to bear away on the other tack.

On the other hand, if the black boat in Fig. 69 turns to starboard, with the wind astern, the boom could suddenly slam over (a gybe), which is tricky enough for the experienced, but for the beginner, in a stiff breeze, could dis-mast or capsize her.

It is clearly stated in the regulations (17), that the vessel not giving way 'shall keep course and speed'. If you must take avoiding action to save yourself, because the other vessel is obviously not going to give way to you, this rule is simply to re-enforce the point that if the regulations state that it is not up to *you* to give way, and you then start to dither about like an anxious old lady on a traffic island, the other chap, not being a mind reader (although ignorant) does not know what action to take, so *you* must decide firmly—and correctly—exactly who gives way to whom, and act accordingly and in sufficient time for the other to see your unmistakable intentions.

If, having taken the fore-going duly into consideration, doubt still remains in your mind, may I remind you once again of what I have already touched on. You should always have on board a horn or klaxon, searchlight or signalling lamp or at least a powerful torch with which you can signal:–

.   1 = I am altering my course to starboard
..   2 = I am altering my course to port
...   3 = I am operating a stern propulsion

I apologise again for repeating this, but please notice the rather pedantic way in which the words themselves are couched, but it is done–as a seaman expects them to be–quite intentional and meaning just exactly what they say.

Imagine for the moment that you are skipper of, say, a twenty-five ton M.F.V. (Motor Fishing Vessel) on your way to work, and going down river on a fast ebbing spring tide of five knots, and your engines are pushing you through the already moving water at a further ten knots, giving a total movement 'over the ground' of fifteen knots.

Rounding a bend (and giving a prolonged blast of warning) you suddenly see a badly handled vessel blocking your course. This is where your quickness of thought and summing-up of the circumstances comes into it as to which side of her you can just about scrape through. If, though, there is no room to scrape through either end of her, all you can do is to jerk 'maximum revs astern' with one hand, and give three short blasts of klaxon or flashes of light with the other, and gently bend your head in prayer, as there is little else (apart from dropping a kedge over the stern and risking life and limb with a cable suddenly going from slack to violin-string tension in a second,) that you can do.

Your three blasts or flashes do not mean 'I am going astern', but 'My engines are going astern', and as the momentum behind twenty-five tons is considerable, and even if going absolutely full astern at maximum power, you will not only have to stop your ten knot speed through the water, but will have to be going astern

SAILING VESSELS APPROACHING EACH OTHER (Rule 12)

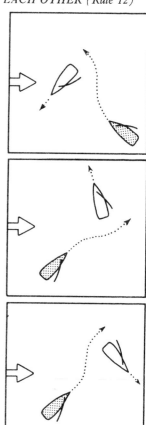

When the wind is on different sides of
each vessel, then the one with the wind
on its PORT (L.H.) side shall give way
to the other.

Fig. 67

When the wind is on the same side of
BOTH vessels, then the vessel nearest
to the wind shall give way to the other.

Fig. 68

When both vessels are 'running free',
(i.e. with the wind astern) then the
vessel with the wind on its PORT side
shall give way.

Fig. 69

POWER VESSELS APPROACHING EACH OTHER

The power vessel with the other power vessel on its STARBOARD (R.H.) side shall give way to the other.

Fig. 71

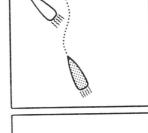

The overtaking vessel keeps clear of the overtaken vessel.

Fig. 72

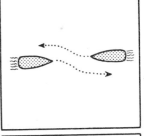

When approaching each other head on, both vessels shall alter course to STARBOARD.

Fig. 73

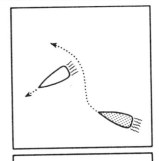

Most know that steam gives way to sail, but a 250,000 ton tanker cannot give way to a 20 foot motor-boat or a 16 foot sailing-dinghy, and probably won't.

Fig. 74

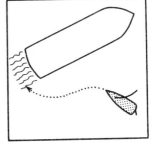

through the water at a full five knots before your boat is stationary *over the ground*.

It is easy, and somewhat trite, for someone to say that you were going too fast around a blind bend where you knew (or should have known) that you would have difficulty in stopping, but after all, be fair, you were going to work as usual, and you did not expect to find a boat completely blocking the sea-way.

There are very many commuters on sea as well as land, remember, and you do not expect someone to have dug a great hole in the road outside your house, or to have re-directed a one-way street *without due notice in the appropriate papers*. You know what you feel like and say to yourself when a learner is trying to do a U-turn, (not very well) on your favourite shot-cut to work in the morning, and you're already late.

Shrug your shoulders, and hope no harm is done. Everyone has to learn some time, so let's try to be constructive and save both our ulcers and our paint-work, but please be patient, and give at least a reasonable chance to the chap who is trying to be as good a seaman as you are–(or are you?)

I sincerely hope you will admit, at least, to being like Sir Francis Drake of one era, or Sir Alec Rose of another–you haven't learned it all yet, and you probably never will, but you can try.

NINE

Semaphore and Morse

SEMAPHORE is basically the best and simplest of the three main communicating codes used at sea, but it suffers from the disadvantage of only being usable in daylight, and the difficulties of sending it standing up in a small boat (which one should never do anyway) in any sort of weather. Its range is limited although can be increased considerably by using proper yellow or red diagonal flags and sent from a position where the background (from the observer's point of view) shows up your signals more clearly. In other words use a couple of old dark sweaters if your background is a white sail, orange or red if a dark blue sky is behind you, or your white underpants and vest if you've got red sails in the sunset. Contrasting colours can literally double the range at which your signals can be seen and understood.

Signalling differs from all trite moralistic sermons in that, unlike charity, it is far easier to give than to receive, and all signallers can send for faster than they can receive for the very simple reason that, while the receiver might pick up your 'WH' which are pretty distinctive, the whole word could be which, where, what, why, when, who, while, or even whilst if you like English grammar, but the point is that you *know* what you are sending and trying to guess at the letters he is not sure about.

When practising, if you send at five to eight words (about twenty-five to thirty-five letters) per minute that is quite reasonable (unless both sender and receiver are really proficient, in which case they won't be reading this bit anyway). Be certain to keep your angles accurate, otherwise the chap on the other end might find your message quite incomprehensible. You will soon know, because if you do not receive a 'C' from him at the end of each word, it means that he hasn't understood you so you have to send the word again–and again–and again–until he is with you and the message begins to make sense. So, send it again more slowly, being absolutely meticulous about your angles, and whip your flags from one letter to the other as fast as (reasonably) possible and freeze for about two seconds. A simple way of counting seconds–but one that is surprisingly accurate–is to count seconds by saying to yourself 'one ruddy second, two ruddy seconds, move'.

Translating ourselves to the land, the Honourable Artillery Company (which purely as a matter of interest heads the list of Army Territorials being founded in 1537, and from which the oldest American Army Unit of the Ancient and Honourable Artillery Company of Boston was formed in 1638) the Royal Horse Artillery, and others of the Royal Regiment of Artillery, Gunners of the R.N. and R.M. have many and varied (some quite unprintable) methods of timing the firing of such as the twenty-one gun salutes given from H.M. ships and the Tower of London on cerimonal occasions.

'Down to the seas again', with the tall ships and the sky and all that, the most important semaphore signals used by H.M. Coastguard and others trying to save your life include $\overline{RRRR}$ (remember that the bar over the top means the letters are sent with no space between) which is both arms or flags waved from chest out and back rather like physical jerks and means 'It is dangerous to beach your boat here'. The sender will then generally point in the direction of the nearest safe landing beach, where he will wave one flag or arm vertically up and down, indicating where you can beach in comparative safety.

Apart from these few things, semaphore is much like Morse, in that all you have to do is learn it, and having done that, to practise on every occasion you can. It is rather like riding a bike; you never forget how to do it, but your receiving speed will fall off incredibly quickly, which is one of the reasons that I stress the advisability of corresponding with other small craft and H.M.C.G. whenever the occasion permits. Apart from the safety factor, that someone knows where you are, if the other chap cannot reply because he is not equipped or hasn't bothered to learn semaphore or Morse, he might start to realise one of his inadequacies as a seaman and will go home and start to learn the need to communicate; this might mean the saving of his–or someone else's–life.

A recent example of this was a long -distance swimmer fairly well out to sea who was hit by a powered planing craft with its bows so well up that they could not (or did not take the trouble to) have a look-out who was in a position to see the water in front of them, least of all the small dot of the swimmer's head. Fortunately a seaman's boat was in the vicinity, her flare was instantly spotted, a message was passed with the shore–whether by semaphore or Morse matters little–the point is that emergency services were told of what had happened and that medical help would be urgently needed and the swimmer is (as far as I know) still alive to tell the story. If that boat had not been able to communicate with the shore several miles away, that man might have died.

As the on-looker who saw it all happen said to me, 'I wonder even if the fools knew what they had done, and even if they did, whether they knew enough to do anything about it.' That, really, is a pretty damming thing to say so deep-heartedly about someone who has just paid several thousand pounds for a powerboat and was 'having a quick run round the bay'. Any man with any sea-time in bemoans the type of ignorance at sea that would not be tolerated on land, but please let us put it right by education and not by legislation.

THE MORSE CODE

Whilst flag and semaphore codes have changed in meaning since their conception, the Morse code has hardly altered at all since its invention in 1837. It was the result of five years work by the American, Samuel Morse, who was pondering on the idea of using electricity 'for the transmission of intelligence' while he was on his way by ship back to the U.S. after having studied in England.

Although to the beginner it seems quite impossible that you will ever get the hang of it, you will be surprised how soon you will at least learn the alphabet if you start learning one letter at a time. For example, you have two out of the twenty-six for a start, as surely you know the famous S.O.S. which is $\cdots$ $---$ $\cdots$, so that only leaves twenty-four. The next priority after S.O.S. is $\overline{XXXXX}$ which is the urgent signal and has priority over all calls except S.O.S., and means that while you are not actually at that moment in danger of life and limb, a situation is developing or deteriorating and you think that someone ought to be told about it. The signal itself has got rather a nice sound to it (unless you are sending it on your own behalf) as $X = -\cdots-$, so your full urgent signal is $-\cdots--\cdots--\cdots--\cdots--\cdots-$

Two Morse signals that you must treat with reserve are 'G' Golf, because if you send that singly $(--\cdot)$ you might well find a pilot steaming towards you with a bill in his hand, as you have called him out by legal means and he can properly charge you for his time and money. The other Morse signal to watch carefully in order to avoid confusion is 'A' Alpha, which, when repeated $\overline{AAA}$ is the general call-up sign to another vessel or shore station. But if you have a diver down, apart from the fact that you should be flying the divers' flag, if a vessel is approaching and there appears to be a danger of injury to your diver, I would not send 'A' as he might simply think you are calling him up and he'll answer in a minute when he gets round to it. Under those circumstances I would be inclined to send 'U' $\cdots-$, 'You are running into danger'. This same signal might be sent to you and it is a signal that should always be taken very seriously. Heave-to, study water, weather, waves, and your position on the chart, and if you still see nothing, turn slowly or go astern and head away from it, but never ignore the signal as it means just exactly what it says.

This is where your full knowledge of Morse—no matter how slow—will come in, as you can ask the sender for the reason for his signal.

Your boat's name should also trip off your tongue in Morse as easily as your own name, particularly as at night you might well be called up with 'CS' (Charlie–Sierra) 'What is your name and number' from the waterguard of Customs and Excise, or H.M. Coastguard, or on certain parts of the coast an R.N. patrol vessel might well want to know who you are, and what are you doing there in the middle of the night.

TEN

Watchdogs of the Seas

I must admit that it seems a little odd to write about watchdogs when referring to the sea, but possibly it helps to describe the organizations whose work is to assist, protect, lead or rescue you at sea. Their jobs are very different, but they can be compared to those watchdogs who welcome friends and guide the stranger, those who silently watch and warn of intruders, those who quietly patrol but can, when required, confront one with extremely sharp teeth, and those who, knowing the dangers ahead, set out into bad weather to help the injured or lost–but in their case small kegs of brandy are not tied around their necks like St Bernards!

TRINITY HOUSE

LIGHTHOUSES

Trinity House is the senior of the three lighthouse services of the British Isles, but the name does not derive from that, but from their name of 'Guild of the most blessed and glorious Trinity and Saint Clement' given with their Charter by Henry VIII in 1514, although they had been a benevolent Society with almshouses for seamen for some considerable time before this. As a matter of interest, part of their petition to the King advised the prevention of foreigners, including 'Scots, Flemish and Frenchmen from learning the secrets of the King's streams'.

In those days, most lighthouses were leased to private individuals for their own gain in tolls, and many of them very indifferently organized, and although in 1594 the Lord High

Admiral's control of beacons and buoys was transferred to Trinity House, it was not until 1836 that they were authorized to buy out all privately-owned lights, although there are still a few, some limited companies, some quite ancient trusts (such as Caernarfon in North Wales for example) who maintain their own.

Nowadays there is much co-operation and sometimes on-the-spot practical planning meetings and consultations with ship owners and their captains. There is an annual meeting held in London consisting of the Elder Bretheren of Trinity House representing England, Wales and the Channel Islands, the Northern Lighthouse Board catering for the needs of Scotland and the Isle of Man, and the Irish Lights commissioners.

When the Irish commissioners were confronted with the partition of Ireland into Eire and Ulster in 1921, they adopted the eminently sensible and successful compromise of increasing their numbers to give fair representation for both countries commensurate with the number of lights and the work-load concerned, and North and South have worked happily together ever since.

Light dues are scaled on the net registered tonnage of vessels entering any ports of the British Isles as an 'earning ship' and sometimes this has to be levied twice, as for example if a liner

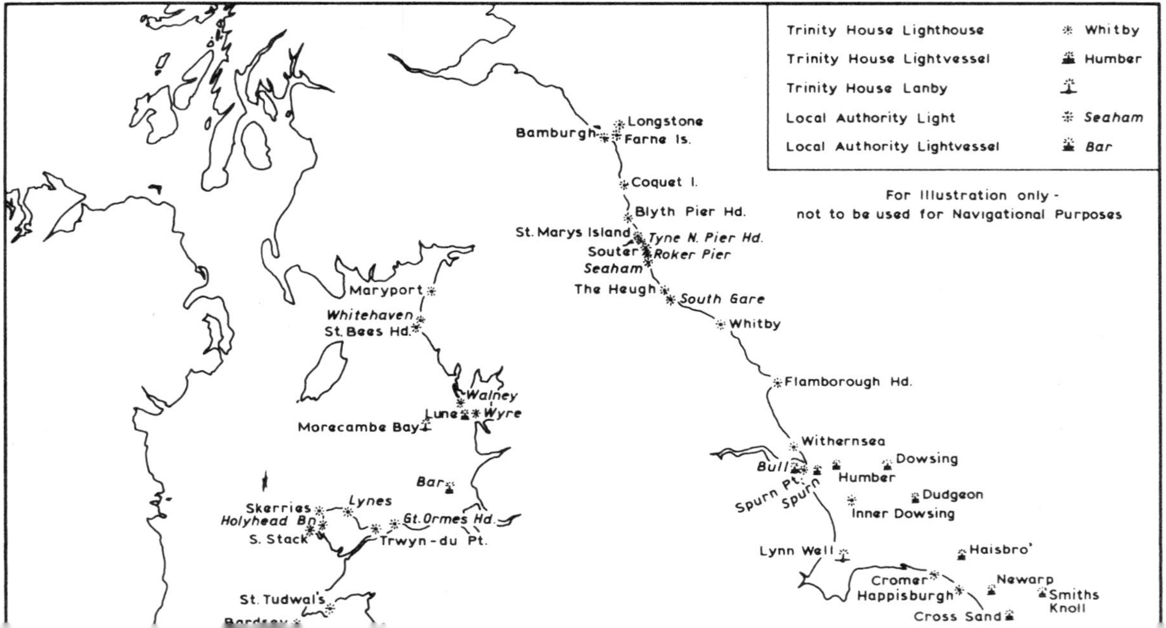

Trinity House Lighthouse ☀ Whitby
Trinity House Lightvessel ▲ Humber
Trinity House Lanby ⚓
Local Authority Light ☀ Seaham
Local Authority Lightvessel ▲ Bar

For Illustration only -
not to be used for Navigational Purposes

Bamburgh☀ ☀Longstone
☀Farne Is.
☀Coquet I.
☀Blyth Pier Hd.
☀Tyne N. Pier Hd.
St. Marys Island☀ ☀Souter
Seaham☀ Roker Pier
The Haugh☀ ☀South Gare
☀Whitby
☀Flamborough Hd.
☀Withernsea
Dowsing▲
Bull▲ Humber▲
Spurn Point ⚓Dudgeon
Spurn Spit Inner Dowsing▲
Lynn Well⚓
Haisbro'⚓
Newarp▲
Cromar☀ ▲Smiths Knoll
Happisburgh☀
Cross Sand▲

Maryport☀
Whitehaven☀
St. Bees Hd.☀
Moracambe Bay☀ Walney
Luna☀ ☀Wyre
Bar▲
Lynas☀ St.Ormes Hd.
Skarries☀ Trwyn-du Pt.
Holyhead B☀
S. Stack☀
St. Tudwal's☀
Bardsey☀

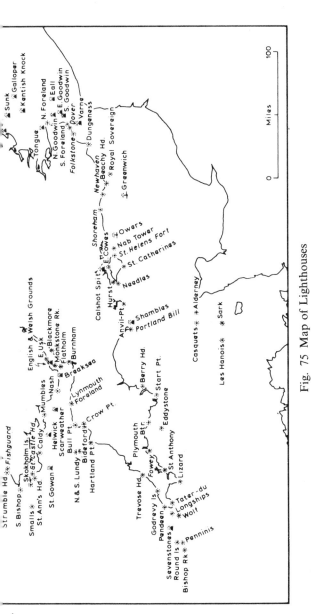

Fig. 75 Map of Lighthouses

embarks passengers at Dublin and more passengers and/or cargo at Liverpool on her way to cruise in the Norwegian fiords. Another unfortunate anomoly is that professional fishing vessels are understandably exempt, but when this was decided, it is very doubtful if anyone ever envisaged the comparatively huge fishing factory canning ships on the high seas today. The Royal Navy, and of course, the Royal Yatch are also exempt.

Trinity House has the ultimate responsibility for fair and equitable division of this income between the three services, which is somewhat complicated by the fact that while the Irish get fewer large ships berthing in her ports, so she could only mathematically demand around 5 per cent of the total income, their commitments are well over half that of Trinity House itself, and almost twice that of her Scottish sister service.

However, luckily for 'they that go down to the sea in ships', the members of all three Services realise that their primary function is to safeguard human life, and that that function comes before any other consideration–financial, political, religious or parochial.

Most of the ninety-three lighthouses, twenty-seven lightvessels, and 700 buoys (of which nearly 400 are lighted) come eventually under the aegis of the elder bretheren of Trinity House, of whom the Master is H.R.H. The Duke of Edinburgh, but apart from this, they also take a prominent and very active part in The International Association of Lighthouse Authorities, where meetings are held in Paris, and European countries can raise matters pertinent to them and their neighbours, and the association tries to solve problems of, for example, one-way traffic systems in restricted and dangerous waterways, shifting sandbanks and any other potential hazards common to seamen.

The differing histories of these three very individual services make fascinating reading, and give one a clearer insight into the type of character necessary to man some of the more solitary 'outposts of the lighthouse empire'. Not only must they be men of the equable temperament necessary to spend weeks in very close proximity of others, but they must also have the individuality and recourcefulness to make, repair or improvise as necessary, whether

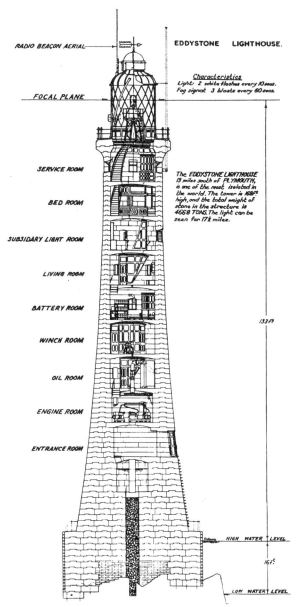

RADIO BEACON AERIAL

EDDYSTONE LIGHTHOUSE.

Characteristics
Light: 2 white flashes every 10 secs.
Fog signal: 3 blasts every 60 secs.

FOCAL PLANE

SERVICE ROOM

BED ROOM

The EDDYSTONE LIGHTHOUSE
is miles south of PLYMOUTH,
is one of the most isolated in
the world. The tower is 133ft
high, and the total weight of
stone in the structure is
4668 TONS. The light can be
seen for 17½ miles.

SUBSIDARY LIGHT ROOM

LIVING ROOM

BATTERY ROOM

WINCH ROOM

133 ft

OIL ROOM

ENGINE ROOM

ENTRANCE ROOM

HIGH WATER LEVEL

16 ft

LOW WATER LEVEL

Fig. 76 Eddystone Lighthouse

the emergency be a blocked loo, agonising toothache, an erratic generator, a broken window or a broken bone. It's all the same, they are on their own, particularly if bad weather prevents relief by ship or helicopter. I never met Gunga Din personally, but these are better men than I am.

Lighthouses are constantly becoming more sophisticated with their use of electronics for fog detection and warnings, in the car-type sealed beam system of reflector lenses, and above all the remote control methods stretching man's recourcefulness to the limit to obtain the essential 100 per cent reliability under all conceivable conditions.

The close co-operation between the three authorities ensures that, apart from a few small fixed lights generally ashore, the intermittent code of sequence and/or colour is not repeated within any reasonable radius, to the effect that the mistaken identity of a major light can quite confidently be taken to be the fault of the osberver–(providing your chart is up-dated) and not that of the lighthouse keeper!

A great step forward has been the introduction of the large automatic navigation buoy (LANBY for short). These are built ashore and towed to their selected position rather like an oil-rig, and present ones like *Royal Sovereign* off Eastbourne weigh around eighty tons when ballasted and are about forty feet in diameter. They have extremely powerful lights, fog warning devices and radar pick-up arials, and altogether form a logical compromise between the lighthouse and the lightvessel.

Lightvessels are usually employed where the seabed is unsuitable for the support of a solid lighthouse weighing anything upwards of 2,500 tons, and are held by an anchor weighing nearly five tons to which she can lay up to *a quarter-mile of chain cable*, and she also carries a spare for emergencies.

As these lightvessels are not self propelled and rely entirely on their mooring, I leave it to your imaginations–and admiration–of what it must be like out there, with the forty-foot waves coming at you and the scudding spray hitting you like shrapnel by winds approaching a hundred knots.

THE PILOT SERVICE

One of the earliest duties of this Ancient Guild of Seamen now known simply as Trinity House was to encourage those who were willing to 'take the labour and advantage of learning the shipmen's craft on the high seas'. Then followed a period of gradual growth, during which time they put their hand to almost everything nautical, including becoming embroiled in wars, particularly those threatening London from the sea. The 1894 Merchant Shipping Acts formally recognized Trinity House's right to examine candidates for the Pilot Service, and to charge vessels dues for their services and penalties for–for example–under-rating tonnage, or flying the 'H' (Hotel) flag (qv) when they were without a pilot qualified for those waters on board.

The Pilot Service, like the Lighthouse Service, is not aided by the state, and its income is derived from a levy on pilot's fees (which in many cases are pooled) but are laid down by Act of Parliament, although pilots are almost invariably self-employed. Trinity Houses raises a levy from the income and charges the pilot for his licence, but as there are about 500 of them in the London district alone, and some 400 ships per day pass through the Straits of Dover–the most crowded waterway in the world, you can see the necessity for thorough and impeccable qualifications.

To be even considered for a pilot, apart from 100 per cent physical fitness, the candidate must have possessed a foreign-going Master Mariner's Certificate and been a watch-keeping officer for at least eight years, and must still be under thirty-five! (Until only just prior to the last war he also had to be competent under sail). That is–reverting to slang– certainly going some. Even then, if he passes the interview by T.H., he must still spend up to six months *at his own expense*, accompanying a qualified pilot on his chosen 'parish', before he can apply for an examination by Trinity House, which, if successful, entitles him to be a Pilot Third Class, to take ships drawing no more than fourteen feet. Pretty strict, I think you will agree, and further examinations take place to be Second, then First class Pilot, so if you ever meet a First Class Pilot, you could literally show him a handful of mud, and he'd probably be able to tell you where you got it from. With all this experience, it is necessary in the Thames, and in some other ports, to have two Pilots, and Senior Pilots at that, so you can imagine the song 'Sailing Down the River on a Sunday Afternoon' is not exactly their signature tune.

It makes one realize the complications of constantly moving sandbanks, the effect of wind on a big ship and their dreaded inability to avoid a collision without going aground themselves because of the narrow channel and the bends in it combined with their length and draught. Faced with that, what would you do?

The proven answer is in the Trinity House system of selection and examination, and it is aimed at the sort of men who can take that type of split-second decision well knowing that if their decision is wrong, the effect of their action could be the loss of possibly thousands of lives in a big liner, or many millions of pounds, but that is the sort of men they are.

The old procedure of a Pilot Cutter waiting 'on station' (which you will sometimes see marked on older charts) is dying out due to the wear and tear on men and boats just hanging around like Mr Micawber, waiting for something to turn up. Most modern vessels radio to Trinity House, or some to a private pilot company if they so wish, give their estimated time of arrival at a predetermined rendezvous, a fast launch delivers the pilot aboard, and another sea journey comes to a safe conclusion, largely through the efforts over the years and the imagination of those men who literally put sign posts or guides on almost every corner of our islands.

H.M. CUSTOMS and EXCISE.

Many famous men of times past were excisemen, including Chaucer in about 1360, Samuel Pepys around 1650, and Burns in 1789. They all left the service, whether voluntarily or not I do not know, neither do I know if there be any moral behind the fact that they didn't stay long.

However, the revenue men, as they were then known, had their regular running fights against smugglers, amounting in many cases to an 'us versus them' campaign, frequently involving,

particularly in the West Country, whole villages surrounding the tiny fishing coves, and escalating almost to small local wars, with spies and informers on both sides.

The principal of import control is anything but a new conception. For hundreds of years it has meant simply that the crown or government raised a tax or levy on the import of certain goods which the public wanted to buy, and would continue to buy even with the added tax. Politically these controls are sometimes instituted where the goods concerned are in direct opposition to our own employment of labour or natural resources. The third, and possibly most vital case for control is where the imports could be physically or morally harmful, or where they could affect public health or environment.

So, in any case, crown or governments have, over more than 300 years–except for a short period of free trade–levied tolls or taxes, and raised a body of men and women to ensure that these levies reach the Royal or governmental purse, that illegal imports were confiscated, and their importers brought to justice.

You can hardly have failed to notice that the main principles of this procedure are the same today as in Chaucer's time over 600 years ago.

However, as mentioned in the section of this chapter dealing with H.M. Coastguard, when the bright lights of smuggling ceased to be worth the candle, the duties of our 'coastal policemen' of the time became sufficiently clear-cut to enable the life-saving–an ever-increasing and specialized task–to be handled by specialists, who subsequently become H.M. Coastguard, and the work of H.M. Custom and Excise–the equally but differently specialized task of ensuring the collection of dues on desirable imports *and* the very strictly limited imports of other items ranging from parrots to porn.

Rabies is the most frightening and repulsive way of dying that I have ever seen (and I've seen a few), and anyone who attempts to evade our laws on the imports of animals is a dangerous and criminal idiot. Any veterinary surgeon will tell you that I am not exaggerating when I say this, and anyone who tries to import cats, dogs, fox-cubs or other carriers of this terrifying disease which has spread into France, and is now only separated from us by the English Channel, deserves the most severe punishment. I am not a very strict moralist, and have sometimes brought over some articles that I should not– but please, not animals. You could be starting an epidemic bigger than you thought possible.

Returning to the more usual side of the work of H.M. Customs, their specially trained branch is the waterguard, and they really are specialists in their briny field, (and if that ain't a mixed metaphor, I don't know what is).

Rudyard Kipling wrote of H.M. Royal Marines as 'Soldier and Sailor Too', but could well have written of the waterguard as 'Taxman and Sailor Too'.

They certainly need to be sailors in no small sense, and to have plenty of guts as well. When duty calls they may have to board a dirty freighter, where neither skipper nor crew speak English (or possibly just make out they don't!), don't want to be held up by customs, and do not feel duty-bound to give assistance to the officers. A couple of officers still have to clamber up a rotten or rusty ladder, possibly in a Force seven or more, with orders to search the ship. The ship might be under suspicion because the officers are acting on information received from Interpol or other sources, it might be just 'a hunch' by local customs or police, or it might well be a purely routine check.

Faced with this prospect, unarmed, and outnumbered eight-to-one or more, most of us would, I think, say 'Not tonight, thanks,

I've got a head-ache', or some other lame excuse to get ourselves off that particular hook.

These men look upon it as part of the job, and do it quietly, efficiently and without fuss, and no public acclaim is given and most certainly is not expected.

Probably your only experience so far with the 'C. and E. ' has been with the scrupulously polite and impeccably dressed members of the service at Dover, Heathrow, Southampton, Liverpool or Gatwick, where all is nicely in the warm. Next time you look at these men, and, nowadays the women who are taking an ever-increasingly responsible part, remember that their next 'draft' might be to replace one of the outside men whose experiences might make *you* go grey overnight.

As a small boat skipper, nipping over the Channel, I will give you no facts on the quantities or articles you may bring back without paying duty, as the quantities of booze and 'baccy' and many other articles, together with the list of countries from which you may bring what, alters frequently.

Your local Customs and Excise officer (he'll be in the phone book), will update you on very recent legislation, but most of the information you will need is contained in Notice No. 8, a facsimile of the front of which is reproduced below (Fig. 77).

This is the document which must be your *Bible* concerning your comings and goings, and remember that, there is a paragraph in the *Small Craft Regulations* (*1953*) which states that certain restrictions shall be placed on vessels of less than forty tons–which probably includes you–which are used outside:–
(a) Twelve miles seaward from that part of the coast of England between Beachy Head and the North Foreland
OR
(b) Thirty-six nautical miles seaward from any other part of the coast of the United Kingdom
     Except any vessel used *exclusively for pleasure*, or as a professional fishing boat, or assisting a vessel in distress.

There are also such things as Store Books, for a long cruise in foreign waters, and the Forms C142 and 142A which concern 'The

Notice to Owners and Masters of British Yachts and Other Private Craft

Her Majesty's Customs and Excise

Fig. 77 Customs and Excise Notice No. 8

declaration of goods obtained abroad or during a voyage'. You might well throw the form over the side, saying 'That does't mean me', but many unfortunates have honestly thought that it didn't mean them, but it did. All that happened, for example, was that their cylinder-head cracked, and it was a Peugot, or Volvo, or Mecedes, it was replaced, and they thought that that was the end of the matter when they had paid the bill and sailed away, but as the old song says, 'That ain't necessarily so'. Regardless of the circumstances, you have *imported* a cylinder head, and depending on when you bought it, and whether it was from a Common Market Country or a member of E.F.T.A., *could*, under certain circumstances, make your cylinder-head liable for import duty, or could be free, but you must declare it, or any rope, canvas or other boat gear bought.

At the same time, I should obtain from the Customs Officer the current list of restrictions and prohibitions–some temporary, because of outbreaks of diseases animal, vegetable or mineral, in the places you are going to or will have arrived from.

The chapter on flags and signals explains the essential use of flag 'Q' Quebec, and you would be wise not to permit your guests or crew to put foot on land until the Customs Officer comes aboard, or if he isn't watching and waiting for you when you secure or moor to a jetty, you–and no-one else–should go ashore and report your presence to the customs.

Finally, if you really want to drive your local and –hitherto–friendly waterguard officer into a complete frenzy of activity (and eventually either a decrease in, or a rapid greying of, the hairs on the heads of your bank manager, accountant or solicitor), all you have to do is to sail into harbour flying 'Q' showing you have been abroad, and with a Christmas tree on your fo'c'sle, a cat sitting on the top talking to a parrot, a dog lubricating the lower branches which shelter a gentleman wearing a turban and surrounded by a distinct aura of opium smoke. Harems *may* be admitted with valid passports, but enquire first about work permits!

If being filmed for 'A' certificate, you should fire a few pistol shots into the air, (safe-guarding your new wristwatch from damage,) whilst reading a dirty book. Just to complete the picture, you could have unused bonded stores and have forgotten to tie a knot in your ensign. I am not pulling your leg about those last nine words, as they are true, although in my years at sea I have never seen it done, although I would love to do it myself just to see what happened, but it is, some say law, some say tradition, of what you *should* do.

Fame and infamy are close, as humour is to tears, or bathos is to pathos, and ignorance can have nasty consequences if you try to play the fool with H.M. Customs and Excise, because whilst you *might* get away with something once, or even twice, the service is sophisticated and very professional. In case you are thinking of C. S. Forrester's *Hornblower* and the revenue cutter mentioned, just remember that a sister-ship of a revenue cutter (1975 edition) recently won a prize in the Cowes–Torquay Powerboat Race, so don't be a twit, as you can't beat 'em, join 'em, and play the game straight.

A very good friend of mine, an ex senior C.I.D. officer was remarking on the fact that I had said that I had seldom seen anyone at an airport or seaport taken away for questioning and/or search, who reappeared except under escort, or with a much slimmer wallet or a notice of intended prosecution. My friend said that it was not exactly due to the fact that C. and E. officers had a crystal ball.

He explained that when he first became a detective, and became accustomed to the interrogation of suspects, after a while, a 'little bell would ring in his head' (his words, not mine), when the suspect told a lie.

The trouble with so much police work, he explained, is that when the questioner asks, for example, 'Were you in the High Street at around 10 p.m. on Saturday last?', and the suspect says 'No'–and the little bell rings, the suspect could be lying because he's been to visit his girl-friend before going home to his wife, he might be selling a watch which 'fell off the back of a lorry', in short he could be lying for any one of a hundred reasons which have nothing to do with the particular case that this detective officer is investigating. When a customs officer looks you in the eye, and utters the well-known question 'Have you anything to declare?', or when out on the briny, a twenty knot (plus) customs launch requests you to heave-to, and asks you politely 'Excuse me, Sir, what are you doing here in this little cove at this time of night . . .?', if your answer is a lie, he will know it, and he will know that you are smuggling something–or someone–into the country.

Take my experience if you will, and never think of customs and excise officers as enemies to be evaded on the one hand, or fools on the other.

They are an extremely fair and human service, but if necessary, can be almost ruthlessly painstaking in their enquiries, so be a good boy (or girl), and you will be allowed abroad again . . . some day.

P.S. Don't try to bribe them, they've seen more bottles of illicit brandy than you've had hot dinners.

SEARCH AND RESCUE — S.A.R.
When ashore and requiring the emergency services of fire, police or ambulance, you simply dial 999 and there they are, alongside you, or outside your house, all screaming to a halt within a matter of minutes. May I say with no disrespect to the land emergency services, that the rapidity of their response is only limited by distance on hard road, and is only delayed by traffic signs and signals largely produced on their recommendations. The S.A.R.

services, on the other hand, frequently have to cope with adverse conditions of wind and water, and often have no fixed address to go to.

H.M. Coastguard is the co-ordinating body which receives all maritime distress calls, which they either act on themselves or re-transmit to whichever they consider to be the appropriate medium. Be it the R.N.L.I., R.N. shore establishments, H.M. ships, R.A.F. long range coastal command type aircraft, plus helicopters large and small; river police and harbour authority launches, pilot boats and often local fishermen might turn out to deal with a particular problem. Of course, as with a purely land emergency, fire, police and ambulance with the hospital services are frequently very much involved.

The problems of H.M. Coastguard vary enormously, ranging from a bird-watcher or a pot-holer stuck half-way up a cliff with a rising tide and worsening weather, a damaged yacht in a full gale, a rubber dinghy with a child swept out to sea, a capsized pleasure boat, or a blazing petrol tanker. Oil slicks and other pollution, sand and gravel stealing from the fore-shore, and freak weather conditions are all part of the Coastguard's routine business.

These, and many others are the problems of H.M. Coastguard, where those in need are searched for, found and rescued–very often from the result of their own folly and/or ignorance.

All this finely handled arithmetic of small forces searching over a large area, or large forces searching over a very resricted area is all dealt with by H.M. Coastguard. In order to do this, they are equipped with specially designed Land-Rovers and powered, inflatable dinghies and by using their unique–in the true sense of the word–radio frequency often co-ordinate with three or four or more services on the spot, and they do this all round the clock and on every day of the year. It might be a Bank Holiday for you, but it is often headache day for them.

The next thing to get absolutely straight about the S.A.R. services is that to call them *is* a 999 call, and is not the maritime equivalent of the A.A. or R.A.C. 'get-you-home' service.

At home you don't dial 999 when you have a leaking tap or

your car won't start, do you? You either mend it yourself in your own time or call in a plumber or a mechanic who fixes it and you pay him for his services. At sea it is just the same. If your life, or that of someone else, is in serious danger, then by all means put up a flare and flash $\cdots --- \cdots$ but if no-one is in danger of life or limb, you either paddle, make a sail out of a sleeping bag, or just anchor and sit it out. If you do not want to do that, flash 'V' Victor $(\cdots -) = $ I require assistance, and someone will come and bale you out, but they might want paying for their trouble, and for Pete's sake why not? If you've run out of fuel, or haven't an anchor, or have gone aground because you didn't know it was low water springs, why should someone else spend time and money digging you out of your own ignorance? I doubt if you would, or else you would have bought an anchor, or asked someone about the state of the tide, or made sure that your tank was topped up before you went to sea at all.

H.M. Coastguard is a wonderful organization, started as long ago as 1822, then purely as an anti-smuggling service. The history of the Coastguard at this period is as hair-raising as any thriller, and the casualties involved in the pitched battles between coastguards and bands of a hundred or more smugglers bore ample witness to the danger of their job.

The smugglers became amazingly astute and cunning, frequently receiving help (active or passive) from the local populace, so the service had to become that much more astute and cunning and organized to deal with the problems; just one of these was the high price paid for spirits due to the tax upon it. More than one of the stately homes of England had uproarious parties on smuggled French brandy, and when the host might well be the local J.P., you can imagine occasions where the straight course of justice was bent in more ways than one!

However, as in all the best adventure stories, right eventually prevailed, and by the middle 1850's large-scale activities of this type were pretty well under control, and more of the coastguards' time and energies could be spent on life saving and accident prevention and control.

Since its inception, H.M. Coastguard, as it is now proudly

FORM CG 66	H.M. COASTGUARD YACHT AND BOAT SAFETY SCHEME	CLUB OR ASSOCIATION

Type of Craft/Rig:			Length

Colours of:	Hull	Topsides	Sail

Sailing/Fishing No:	Speed and endurance under power

Special identification features:

Life raft type and Serial No:

Dinghy Type and Colour:

Life Jackets carried

Radio   HF/MF   Trans/Rec:

Fitted   VHF   Channels and call sign:

         Other Equipment:

Distress signals — type carried:

PROVIDING A PHOTOGRAPH

Fig. 78 H.M

known, has been controlled in turn by H.M. Customs (in its earliest days) then the Admiralty, the Board of Trade, the Admiralty again during the 1939 to 1945 War, the Ministry of Transport and Civil Aviation, then the Board of Trade again, and is now organized on a highly sophisticated basis by the Marine Division of the Department of Trade.

An excellent no-charge self-help yacht and boat safety scheme known as CG66 has recently been launched, and which I thoroughly recommend for your own life's sake. The full details of your boat are registered with your local coastguard so the HMCG (a) can tell if your boat is stolen while you are not looking, and (b) that if reported overdue, they have a description of your boat,

NAME OF CRAFT

H.M. COASTGUARD

and where name displayed

▌base:

▌mooring:

▌activity (fishing, racing, etc.)

▐sea area(s)

▐Contact's name, address and
▐hone No:

▐r's name, address and
▐hone No:

**THIS PORTION SHOULD BE RETAINED
AND PREFERABLY LEFT ASHORE WITH
SOME RESPONSIBLE PERSON
CONCERNED WITH YOUR SAFETY.**

Signature

▐CRAFT IS ADVANTAGEOUS

▐ Cg 66

together with details of fuel range, radio equipment (if any) life-saving gear carried, anchors, rafts, etc. This form should be renewed annually in case any changes in identification marks or equipment have taken place.

As soon as you get to port you phone your agent and say, for example 'O.K., I'm here now but am pushing on to Flushing and will be there on Monday.' If your agent does not get a call from you early on Tuesday, and particularly if the weather is a bit dicey, he or she gets on the phone to the coastguard, and says in the immortal words of *Mrs Dale's Diary*, 'I'm worried about Jim'. Your agent can then relax because H.M. Costguard will swing into their well-practised search and rescue routine and (DV) Jim will be

K

back home before his wife has had time to get rid of the baker.

Seriously though, that is simply how it works, and it does work–but it can only work if *you* help the coastguard to help you.

ROYAL NATIONAL LIFEBOAT INSTITUTION

When you gotta go, you gotta go is an expression heard in many a context, but few if any, serve adequately to describe these men who at a moment's notice leave their family, home, work, peace and security to face acute discomfort–to put it at its very least–and the risk of a most unpleasant death.

The R.N.L.I. was started in 1824 and has (1975) saved 100,000 lives, commercial and fishing vessels to the cost of £1,225,000, and pleasure craft even more at £1,617,600 from the sea which in its merciless turn has exacted its grim toll of some 400 members of R.N.L.I. crews.

The institution, like the sister organizations which followed our lead in the Netherlands, Western Germany and Sweden is entirely self-supporting and one often hears the simple question asked 'Why?'

The answer is not so simple, except from the bald fact that the proof of the pudding is in the eating, and it is difficult to explain why the whole spirit would drop out of the organization, and that a lifeboat service run from Whitehall would be disastrous for the *esprit de corps* of the thousands of helpers–apart from crews. In the last century a grant was made to the R.N.L.I. by the government for several years, and it rapidly became obvious that any form of central control wherever based nationally, must be remote from some station somewhere which had problems peculiar to itself which were not understood at head office. The service reverted to its previous self-supporting economy, and so it stays today, with a large amount of autonomy resting with each station which engenders its own loyalty. With 133 deep-sea lifeboats backed up by over 100 inflatable inshore lifeboats, some capable of speeds approaching thirty knots, the R.N.L.I. covers up to about thirty miles off the shores of the whole of the United Kingdom, including the Irish Republic and the Channel Islands, and encompasses some of the most dangerous and certainly the busiest sea-lanes in the world. (See Fig. 80).

Each patch of water has different characteristics under different circumstances, and these local circumstances are well known by the local lifeboat committee. All the local machinery of lifeboat control and administration is vested in the Hon. Secretary or his deputy, often a retired experienced mariner, who is appointed by the committee of management of the R.N.L.I.

All operational matters come under the control of the Hon. Secretary, together with H.M. Coastguard, but it is the Hon. Secretary or his deputy who alone take the responsibility for the order to launch or to stand fast.

This will explain what puzzles many landsmen when they hear of a lifeboat from 'X' being called to 'Y' when there appears to be a nearer lifeboat at 'Z', but the local secretaries know their waters and they know after rapid phone conferring that 'Z' harbour entrance is impassable at low water springs, or the Force 10 is blowing straight from the north east making launching too dangerous, or that exposed rocks make it quicker for another station to head straight for the casualty. All factors must be weighed up accurately but quickly before the lifeboat is sent to success or disaster–seldom glory as most of what they do goes unpublished and is accepted as part of the job.

So what do they make out of it? Once at sea, they are paid the sum of two pounds for the first two hours, and fifty pence per hour after that. Usually the only full-time member of the crew is the

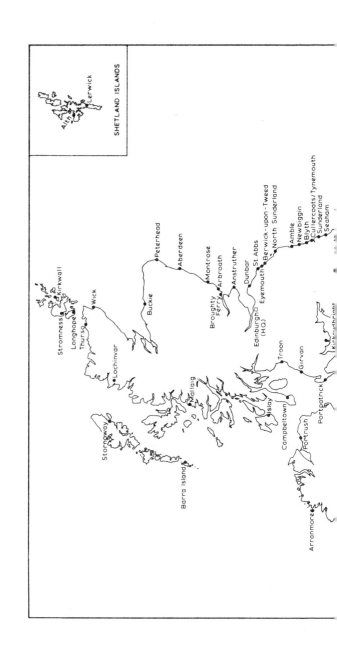

SHETLAND ISLANDS

Lerwick

Kirkwall
Stromness
Longhope
Thurso
Wick

Lochinvar

Peterhead

Aberdeen

Buckie

Montrose
Arbroath
Broughty
Ferry
Anstruther

Dunbar

Edinburgh
(H.Q.)

St Abbs
Eyemouth
Berwick-upon-Tweed
North Sunderland
Amble
Newbiggin
Blyth
Cullercoats/Tynemouth
Sunderland
Seaham

Troon

Girvan

Portpatrick

Kirkcudbright

Mallaig

Islay

Campbeltown

Portrush

Stornoway

Barra Island

Arranmore

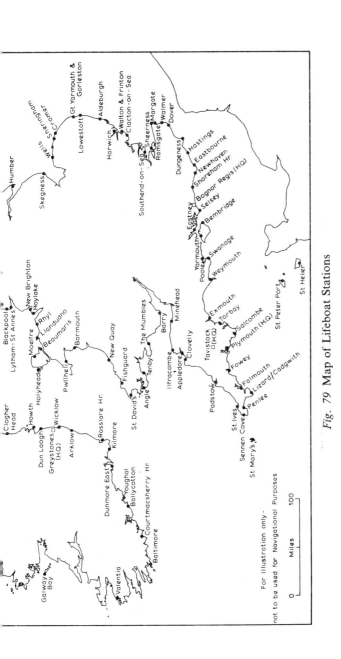

Fig. 79 Map of Lifeboat Stations

For illustration only -

not to be used for Navigational Purposes

0   Miles   100

mechanic or coxswain/mechanic who is a regular employee of the R.N.L.I. and also does maintenance on boathouse and equipment. The coxswain, second coxswain and assistant mechanic also receive small retainers, but as the total salary bill for crews in 1976 will amount to just over £401,000 which, spread over all boats amounts to some £3,015 *per boat per year*, I think you will admit that risking their lives hardly puts them in the supertax bracket! Whilst on the question of money, I think that if there be a best buy for all the many charities registered in this country, surely few can equal the R.N.L.I. where less than a quarter of their income is spent on the administration, printing, advertising, exhibition costs, etc. necessary to raise the vast sums always needed.

If you can afford a boat, you can surely afford to enroll as (at least) a member for a couple of quid a year. They do not ask you if you are a member before they pick you up, and do not send you a bill when they have—even if they've damaged their own boat in the process of saving your life.

What motivates these men to do so much for so many for so little, even they couldn't tell you. It's not the glory, because they get little enough of that and in fact almost all seem to hide from it, and it's not the power because their matter-of-factness dispels that.

I was once in a partially disabled twenty-seven-foot boat in a south west force eight gusting to nine with both wind and tide streams pushing me slowly but inexorably sternfirst onto the Needles rocks, which I, frankly, found most unamusing. My flares were spotted and I was picked up and towed back to safety.

Once the lifeboat was winched back up the slip into the lifeboat house and the doors closed I was given a large mug of tea and a cigarette—and a strange thing happened.

The members of the R.N.L.I. crew took off their uniform life jackets and yellow oilskins and as they started to hang them up I saw for the first time the men underneath—several fishermen and the schoolmaster, the farmworker, the taxi driver—just a group of men chatting quietly about tomorrow's film or football match—the storm howling outside completely forgotten—but not by me!

ELEVEN

Important Harbour Signs

ENGLISH	*WELSH*	*FRENCH*
Anchoring prohibited	Dim bwrw angor	Defense de mouiller
Mooring prohibited	Dim angori	Accostage interdit
Customs Office	Swyddog toll	Douane
Harbourmaster	Harbwrfeistr	Capitaine de Port
Hospital	Ysbyty	Hopital
Garage	Garej	Garage
Boat Chandler or Engineer	Masnachwr cychod	Fournisseur de Marine

GERMAN	*DUTCH*	*SPANISH*
Ankern verboten	Verboden ankerplaats	Fondeadero prohibido
Anlegen verboten	Verboden aan te leggen	Amarradero prohibido
Zolamt	Douanekantoor	Aduana
Hafenkapitans	Havenkantoor	Comandancia de puerto
Krankenhaus	Zeikenhuis	Hospital
Garage	Garage	Garaje
Yachtruster	Scheepsleverancier	Almacen navales

Signal Index

Flag	Meaning of flag hoisted singly	Morse	Semaphore Him to you	Semaphore You to him	Special meanings in morse and semaphore	Phonetic
A*	I have a diver down; keep well clear at slow speed	· —	↘	✓	Sem: AAA = Call up signal. Does not have same meaning as flag. If required send Morse UNIFORM	ALFA
B*	I am taking in, or discharging or carrying dangerous goods (e.g. patrol or explosives)	— · · ·	↑	↓	Flag might have central white circle = usually carrying motor spirit in barge or small coaster	BRAVO
C	"YES" (Affirmative) or "The meaning of my previous groups of signals is in the affirmative"	— · — ·	↗	↘	Sem: = Word received. "Yes" is spelt out in full Morse: = "Yes" (Affirmative)	CHARLIE OR SHARLIE
D	Keep clear of me, I am manoeuvring with difficulty	— · ·	·→	→·	Sem: = (when wagged up and down) "It is safe to land your boat here"	DELTA
E*	I am directing my course to Starboard	·	↘	↗	Sem: EEE = "Erase my last word"	ECHO
F	I am disabled. Communicate with me	· · — ·	↓	↑	Morse: = as flag signal	FOXTROT
G	I require a Pilot. When made by fishing vessel operating at sea means "I am hauling nets, keep clear"	— — ·	↙	↘	Morse by light or horn is same as flag signal (except near Port)	GOLF

Flag	Meaning of flag hoisted singly	Morse	Semaphore Him to you	Semaphore You to him	Special meanings in morse and semaphore	Phonetic
H	I have a pilot on board	· · · ·			Usually flown at Port yard-arm. Never sent by morse as a single letter unless meaning "What the heck are you doing?"	<u>H</u>OTEL
I *	I am directing my course to Port	· ·				<u>I</u>NDIA
J	I am on fire and have dangerous cargo on board. Keep well clear of me	· – – –				<u>JULIETT</u>
K	I wish to communicate with you	– · –			Morse as flag signal but usually made obvious by various means	<u>K</u>ILO
L *	You should stop your vessel instantly	· – · ·				<u>L</u>IMA
M	My vessel is stopped and making no way through the water	– –				<u>M</u>IKE
N	"NO" (Negative) or "The meaning of my previous group of signals is in the negative"	– ·			Sem: Spell out word "NO"	NO<u>V</u>EMBER
O *	Man overboard	– – –			Morse as signal flag	<u>O</u>SCAR

Flag	Meaning of flag hoisted singly	Morse	Semaphore Him to you	Semaphore You to him	Special meanings in morse and semaphore	Phonetic
P	In Harbour: "All should report - about to proceed to sea" At sea by fishing vessels: My nets are caught"	· — — ·				PAPA
Q	"My vessel is healthy and I request free pratique"	— — · —				QUEBEC
R	No special meaning allotted. (Possibly to avoid mistake for several similar National Ensigns)	· — ·			Sem: R̄R̄R̄ = "It is dangerous to beach your boat here." Morse: "Message received and understood".	ROMEO
S	"My engines are going astern"	· · ·			Morse: As flag signal	SIERRA
T	"Am engaged in pair trawling" (Do not sail between vessels)	—			Morse: "Word received and understood". On continental coasts often with green flares.	TANGO
U	You are running into danger	· · —			Sem: As flag signal Morse: As flag signal VOCIFEROUS SIGNAL WHICH MEANS JUST WHAT IT SAYS!	UNIFORM
V	I require assistance	· · · —				VICTOR
W	I require medical assistance	· — —				WHISKEY

Flag	Meaning of flag hoisted singly	Morse	Semaphore Him to you	Semaphore You to him	Special meanings in morse and semaphore	Phonetic
X*	Stop carrying out your intentions and watch for my signals	–··–			Morse: XXX = URGENT and is the next priority after S.O.S.	X-RAY
Y*	I am dragging my anchor	–·––				YANKEE
Z	I require a tug. By fishing vessels operating: I am shooting nets	––··				ZULU
					CODE AND ANSWER	

Substitutes THIRD letter in hoist of four

"SOXISIX"

"SETTESEVEN"

"OKTOATE"

"NEVONINER"

"ZERO"

Substitutes SECOND letter in hoist of four

6

7

8

9

0

"UNAWUN"

"BEESOTOO"

"TERRATHREE"

"CARTERFOR"

"PANTAFIFE"

Substitutes FIRST letter in hoist of four

1

2

3

4

5

GLOSSARY OF SOME COMMON NAUTICAL TERMS AND ABBREVIATIONS USED IN THIS BOOK

ABEAM	At right angles to line of keel.
AFT	Towards the stern of vessel.
ANCHOR BUOY	Small buoy attached to anchor to give both position and additional means of recovery.
ASTERN	Behind the vessel.
ATHWART	From side to side.
BATTEN DOWN	To fasten all openings, hatches, sky-lights etc.
BEACON	Lighted or unlighted aid to navigation set on shore or rocks.
BEAM	Maximum width of vessel.
BEAM ENDS	Vessel forced onto her sides.
BELAY	To make a rope fast.
BIGHT	Any part of a rope between its ends.
BILGES	Bottom inside of vessel where water collects.
BOWER	Main anchor, carried forward on vessel.
CABLE	Nautical measurement 100 fathoms = 200 yards = 1/10 of a nautical mile.
CLEW	Corner of sail where leech meets the foot.
COURSE	The direction a vessel steers in.
DEAD RECKONING	Position calculated from course, distance covered.
DRAFT	Depth of water occupied by a vessel.
EBB	Period when tide flows from the land.
ENSIGN	Flag denoting vessel's nationality.
FATHOM	Nautical measurement of depth—six feet.
FENDER	Rubber or other material hung on hull side to prevent chafe between vessels, or vessel and pier.
FIDDLES	Edging or shaped raised pieces to prevent things sliding or falling off surfaces at an angle.
FLOOD	Period when tide flows towards the land.
GALLEY	The cooking department.
GIMBALS	Two concentric axes enabling compass or stove to remain horizontal at all times.
GREEN SEA	Term used when solid water is shipped aboard.
GROUND	The bottom of the sea.
H.M.C.G.	Her Majestey's Coastguards.
HEADS	Toilet in a vessel.
HEAVE TO	To stop, so vessel has as little directional movement as possible.

HELM	Tiller or wheel for steering.
HOLDING GROUND	How well or badly the bottom holds an anchor.
INSHORE	Towards or near the shore.
JACK STAFF	Small staff in bows for Jack.
KEDGE	Lightweight anchor.
KEDGING	Moving vessel by hauling on warp connected to kedge.
KNOT	One nautical mile per hour.
LANDFALL	Part of coast first sighted by vessel coming from sea.
LEE	Side away from direction of wind, tide etc.
LEEWAY	Sideways drift caused by wind pressure.
LOG	Instrument for measuring distance run.
LOG BOOK	Record of events and navigational notes.
LUBBER LINE	Line inside compass indicating ship's bows.
MIDSHIPS	Centralising rudder; Middle part of vessel.
NEAP TIDES	Smaller rise and fall of a tide. Middle phases of the moon.
OFFING	To seaward.
PORT	Left hand side of vessel looking forward.
RUN	A day's run is distance covered in twenty-four hours.
S.A.R	Search And Rescue.
SPRING	Mooring ropes. Back spring led from forward aft or aft forward.
SPRING TIDES	Greatest rise and fall of a tide, when moon is new or full.
STARBOARD	Right hand side of vessel facing forward.
TILLER	Lever for turning rudder.
UNDER WAY	When vessel is not moored, anchored or made fast.
WARP	Rope for tying up, towing and in small craft, anchoring.
WATCHES	Ship's time in four-hour periods from midnight except for 'First Dog Watch' 4 p.m.–6 p.m. and 'Second Dog Watch' 6 p.m.–8 p.m.

INDEX